easy country

easy country

a new approach to country style

KATRIN CARGILL

photography by SIMON UPTON

RYLAND

PETERS

& SMALL

LONDON NEW YORK

For my mother, in celebration
of her eightieth year, with love

For this edition:
Senior designer Paul Tilby
Senior editor Henrietta Heald
Production manager Patricia Harrington
Art director Leslie Harrington
Publishing director Alison Starling

Main contributor Alison Culliford

First published in 1998
This compact edition published in the UK and
the USA in 2008 by Ryland Peters & Small
20–21 Jockey's Fields, London WC1R 4BW
519 Broadway, 5th Floor, New York, NY 10012
10 9 8 7 6 5 4 3 2 1

Text copyright © Katrin Cargill 1998, 2008
Design and photographs copyright
© Ryland Peters & Small 1998, 2008

A CIP record for this book is available from
the British Library.

Library of Congress Cataloging-in-Publication Data

Cargill, Katrin.
  Easy country : a new approach to country style /
Katrin Cargill ; photography by Simon Upton.
    p. cm.
  Includes index.
  ISBN 978-1-84597-691-0
  1. Decoration and ornament, Rustic. 2. Interior
decoration.--History--21st century. I. Upton,
Simon, 1967- II. Title.
  NK1994.R87C37 2008
  747--dc22

                                     2007047167

PRINTED IN CHINA

contents

introduction

Opposite A lightly limewashed oak table stands centre stage in a simply furnished dining room. The huge mirror introduces a touch of grandeur.

Right The unusual zigzag shape of these square-cut balusters transforms a utilitarian stairway into the decorative focus of a country entrance hall.

Fashions in interior decoration generally change at an alarming pace. Country style, however, has been around for decades and, judging by the wide range of country-style furniture, fabrics and accessories on the market, it still appeals to a huge number of people – perhaps in part because it offers a perfect antidote to the hustle and bustle of the working day and the increasing stresses of modern living.

Country style enjoyed enormous popularity in the 1970s, when no kitchen was complete without its stripped-pine dresser. Over the years, the look has been worked and reworked, absorbing different elements from all over the world, accumulating touches of English, Mediterranean, North American, Scandinavian, Indian and South American style. In the process, country-style furniture has deviated from its original designs, and the colours of country-style textiles and accessories have been exaggerated until the objects or ideas that first inspired them can no longer be easily identified. Modern labour-saving components of kitchens and bathrooms are given a thin veneer of 'rustic' charm so we can pretend that they are relics of a happier, safer, less complicated rural past.

I trace my own love of country style back to my childhood in the Swiss Alps. My most powerful memories are associated with alpine colours and alpine traditions: in spring, the first white crocuses and family rituals at Easter; in summer, brilliant green meadows dotted with bright blue gentians; in autumn, the pine and mushroom scents of the forest; in winter, a cold snow-covered landscape outside and, indoors, the industrious practice of many crafts.

These happy memories provided a solid foundation for my personal interpretation of the style. In our little urban home, I have tried to create a feeling of the country. The walls are clad with wide wooden planks painted in subtle colours. The floorboards have been stripped and painted and are covered with soft cotton runners. The furniture is mainly wooden and painted. During the winter I have a fire burning in the grate, and in summer I grow country flowers in windowboxes so we can have sweet peas and old-fashioned roses in the house.

Opposite Simple wooden-clad walls, solid well-made furniture and a few favourite objects simply displayed will bring a sense of easy country style to any house, whether it is in the centre of a city or buried in the depths of the countryside.

Right Sheer curtains allow light to flood in through the cottage windows.

Easy country is more than a look; it is a way of living. It is all about choosing well-crafted objects made from natural materials that will improve with the years, creating a sense of comfort, continuity and permanence. The new easy country look portrayed in this book is a cleaner, fresher, pared-down style that strips away the frills and unnecessary clutter of the traditional country look and goes back to basics. Thanks to its simplicity and honesty, it will withstand the whims of fashion.

Easy country is not about slavishly recreating the rustic lifestyle of the past. For example, trying to cook over an open fire in a city kitchen would be ridiculous, for modern comforts – central heating, hot water, modern appliances and double glazing – are not incompatible with easy country style. Instead, easy country takes inspiration from the very best of country style – the informal, relaxed, unconstrained atmosphere we associate with rural living and the simple furniture handmade by craftsmen who took great pride in the articles they created.

This book shows you my vision of easy country. It begins by looking at the six key looks that have influenced my interpretation of the style: English country cottage, Shaker, Mediterranean, Swedish, Early American and modern country. From each one I have drawn certain elements, then combined them to create a new country look that is simple, fresh, honest and, above all, comfortable and easy to live with. Later chapters cover the individual elements that characterize easy country – including colours, wall and floor finishes, furniture and accessories. Finally, the 'Rooms' chapter showcases interiors that typify easy country style, helping you to understand how to put the look together and thereby enabling you to create it in your own home.

At the heart of easy country is an easy elegance combined with a supreme comfort that is good to come home to. It is a very distinctive look that is unmistakably rural, but it is also an uncluttered, fresh look that is perfectly at home in an urban setting. Good luck in bringing easy country to your home!

influential styles

All six of the interior styles described in this chapter have greatly influenced the development of my own easy country look. In each case, particular elements appealed to me: the warmth and comfort of the English country cottage; the harmony and balance of Shaker interiors; the light, spacious atmosphere of the Mediterranean; the cool elegance and subdued palette of Swedish country homes; the hardworking honesty of the early American settlers' houses; and the bold simplicity of modern country.

english country cottage

An easy country interpretation of the traditional English country cottage banishes gloom, clutter and confusion and replaces them with a new combination of light and space, simplicity and order, harmony and restraint.

The whitewashed thatched cottage with roses climbing round the door is an archetypal image of the English countryside that is dismissed by some as an uninspiring cliché. However, the appeal of the English country cottage endures – Beatrix Potter's home and William Wordsworth's Dove Cottage in the Lake District and Anne Hathaway's cottage near Stratford-upon-Avon are three of the most visited houses in England. Perhaps this is because all three feed a modern nostalgia for a world of homely simplicity and rustic harmony, a cosy idyll of country living.

In reality, living in a country cottage can be less than idyllic. Cottages were built for labouring folk and were never intended to be luxurious. A traditional cottage had just one room on the ground floor, entered directly from the front door, with basic amenities, although not all such rooms were cheerless. Before the Industrial Revolution, this room would have served both as a working and a living area, where the occupants made a living from cottage industries such as weaving, woodworking and spinning. Furniture would therefore have been restricted to the necessities – a couple of chairs and a table – so it could easily be cleared out of the way to make room for work activities.

Country cottages were often tiny by modern standards, their crooked beams head-skimmingly low, the staircases steep and narrow, rooms dark and poky. Windows were few and far between, partly to exclude wintry draughts and partly because

Above Interior designer Wendy Harrop, the owner of this picturesque cottage, replaced the crowded garden beds with practical gravel paths and an abundance of lavender and old-fashioned roses.

Right A buttery-yellow wash on the rough plaster walls, white-painted beams, loose covers in calico and a well-placed mirror infuse this small room with brightness and light.

This page A pinkish-red antique quilt complements the toile de Jouy covering the headboard and armchair and the cheerful checks of the lampshade, cushion, tablecloth and curtains. The eclectic mix of red and white injects life into this whitewashed bedroom.

Above right A sense of tranquillity and order reigns in this corner of a living room. Despite its usefulness as a storage space, the simple whitewashed side table with its pair of candles in glass storm shades looks elegant and uncluttered.

Above far right A pair of traditional Irish linen tea towels have been recycled as a pair of curtains.

of the tax on windows levied during the 18th century. Easy country style offers solutions to most of these drawbacks. Translucent curtains or simple blinds allow in light and sunshine, while reflective, pale walls in soft country colours – wild rose, moss green, creamy white – make the most of the available light and add a refreshing sense of spaciousness and simplicity.

In the 1970s and 1980s, when country-style interiors first became popular, a desire to recreate the country-cottage look meant that houses were filled with a hotchpotch of Victorian furniture, junk-shop finds, frilly chintzes and flowery wallpapers. Now, however, a new mood of simplicity infuses cottage style. The easy country look replaces floral wallpaper and matching curtains with plastered, painted or wooden walls, and there is new interest in traditional paint finishes such as distemper, which are kinder to old walls that need to breathe. Cotton loose covers and checked cushions have taken the place of fussy tapestries and flouncy, overstuffed furnishings. Wall-to-wall carpets and thick needlepoint rugs have been ousted by stripped, polished or painted boards, chunky, tactile coir matting or smooth, worn stone floors.

Finally, flea market bric-à-brac has been replaced with a few carefully chosen objects. Only one element remains unchanged – a bowl of fresh flowers, loosely arranged, will always evoke the essence of the English countryside.

shaker

The pared-down aesthetic of the Shakers offers a timeless rustic alternative to contemporary minimalism. Indeed, the perfect simplicity and sense of harmony typical of Shaker interiors capture the essence of easy country style.

Left An unassuming clapboard house and barn buried in the woods of Maine conceal an authentic Shaker interior.

Right The sparse, unadorned kitchen contains nothing that is not eminently useful. The generous open shelving is home to a collection of baskets, wooden bowls, earthenware and other country crockery. Recalling American Colonial times, cupboards, doors and window frames are covered in a warm, earthy, barn-red milk paint.

With its simplicity of line and functional beauty, Shaker style has become an American country classic. Out of the enclosed, puritanical, other-worldly community of the Shakers came many devices that we mistakenly think of as products of the 20th century, such as built-in cupboards, swivel chairs and roller-blinds. It is easy to forget, when admiring the sheer beauty, efficiency and grace of Shaker furniture, buildings and objects, that they were designed only to serve, not to decorate.

In 1774, members of the United Society of Believers in Christ's Second Appearing – nicknamed Shakers on account of their shaking devotional dance – arrived in North America from England in pursuit of religious freedom.

Led by Mother Ann Lee, they chose to live a communal life bound by vows of chastity and separation from the world. The Shaker credo 'do not make what is not useful' meant that all unnecessary ornamentation had to be avoided; rather, objects had to embody endurance and efficiency. All pieces had to comply with a strict set of rules – the Millennial Laws – which decreed exactly how everything should be made and how the finished object should look. Everything, down to rivets, nails and tacks, was made in the community, and for this reason each Shaker item was unique.

Shaker creations are a testimony to the meticulous craftsmanship of a people who were unaffected by the whimsical fashions of the outside world. The key to the beauty that emanated from the hands of Shaker craftsmen was Mother

Left A bentwood rocker with sinuous lines and a seat made of tape woven into a chequerboard pattern occupies a corner of the living room. The majority of the objects in the house are original Shaker pieces.

Ann's tenet: 'Do your work as if you had a thousand years to live, and as if you were to die tomorrow.' For the Shakers, excellent workmanship was a form of worship – they strove to achieve the best for the glory of God.

A love of Shaker style need not mean recreating in historical detail the interior of a meeting house, but following a few Shaker 'laws' will bring a new purity to any room. Simple Shaker furniture fashioned from grained woods will bring order and symmetry to sparse, clean

Above The Shakers were renowned for their wonderful craftsmanship and immense practicality. This bank of built-in drawers in slightly graduated sizes is a perfect example of their meticulous handiwork. Yellow milk paint is used on all the woodwork.

Above right This sturdy Shaker desk has been painted an unusual blue-black.

Right A light, airy bedroom has been simply furnished with a high bed and a fine antique quilt.

interiors. White walls can be offset with woodwork painted in blocks of strong, deep blue, dark bay-leaf green, barn red or straw yellow. Windows should be left bare or covered with translucent cotton blinds. Surfaces and floors must be kept free of clutter; items should be hidden in cupboards or hung from the ubiquitous Shaker peg rails. Details such as baskets made from willow or ash splint and chair seats woven from cotton tape complete the picture. Everything has its place, and harmony and order will reign.

mediterranean

Mediterranean country style is all about space, colour, light and shade. Whether you are indoors or out, the sea and the sun are never far away.

The influences that come together to make Mediterranean style stretch from the rugged Atlantic coast of Portugal in the west as far as the Turquoise Coast of Turkey in the east, taking in the wide scoop of the Mediterranean Sea, including the pine-covered, rocky islands of the Aegean, on the way – one glorious swathe of dazzling blue and sun-bright white.

This is a style characterized by openness and spaciousness, whose effect is clean and spare. In warm climates there is no need to build small to keep in the heat of the hearth in winter. Rooms are large and airy, windows are flung wide open to let in the wonderful reflected light typical of seaside locations. Thick stone walls and small shuttered windows are designed not to keep out the cold but to provide relief from the summer heat. In parts of the eastern and southern Mediterranean, houses are built as separate rooms around a central courtyard that serves as a living room, dining room and garden. Food is prepared and preserved in the cool of the kitchen, but eating always takes

Above left A cluster of fisherman's huts has been restored by the interior designer Vera Iachia and her husband Manrico, using indigenous materials to create visual links with the local landscape.

Top A whitewashed bamboo roof shades concrete ledges covered with soft mattresses, creating an inviting retreat from the heat of the midday sun.

Above The veranda has panoramic views of the countryside.

Opposite Outdoors meets indoors in this bright and airy living room with its eclectic combination of old furniture and found objects. The centrepiece is an old rowing boat whose faded colours were the inspiration for the fabric used to cover the sofa. The blue-stained concrete floor set with pebbles also evokes the seashore, while the overhead light fitting strung with pebbles is reminiscent of a lobster pot.

place outside, in a shady spot, where a gentle breeze heightens the appetite for robust, delicious flavours.

Whether houses are built of stone or other local materials such as reeds or mud, their shape is organic. Bare rock, thick plaster and layer after layer of whitewash create undulating, uneven walls with a rough-hewn, monolithic, almost sculptural quality. Floors are hard and cool – consisting of terracotta tiles, stone, smoothed concrete or raw, unpolished marble – and frequently covered with simple cotton mats that feel comfortable underfoot.

Modern technology makes it possible for us to recreate the Mediterranean country style in cooler northern climes. Central heating and improved insulation systems mean that large rooms, roughly plastered walls and hard, cool floors are compatible with the comforts – in particular, warmth and cleanliness – that we expect in today's homes.

Limewash, the oldest of all paints, is still the traditional finish for exteriors across the Mediterranean region. It takes several coats to create an opaque layer of colour, but walls are re-limewashed often, usually every spring, to hide any ravages wrought by winter weather. The warm, rich, intense, colours traditionally associated with the region – umber and ochre in Italy, vibrant blue in Greece, spicy dark reds in North Africa – are gradually faded and bleached by the

Right One cottage serves as a kitchen and breakfast area. The contemporary stainless-steel oven is complemented by an open fire, used for grilling fish freshly caught from the sea.

Below All the items in this corner are made from natural materials: a massive wooden table, woven chair backs and seats, a straw lampshade and a huge shallow basket holding fresh fruit and vegetables.

Opposite, above Whitewashed walls and ceilings and woodwork painted a clear, vibrant blue add light and colour to a bathroom.

Opposite, below The seaside theme is continued in this airy bedroom.

powerful summer sun until they become the familiar chalky hues that are so strongly reminiscent of sea, sand and earth. Some modern paints offer an instantly faded, mellowed effect, allowing you to recreate an impression of the sunbleached Mediterranean no matter where you live.

Mediterranean houses are clean and neat, but never clinical. Every morning, floors are given a sweep or sloshed down with a bucket of water, and mats and rugs are beaten vigorously. Then, when the sun rises high in the sky and the heat of the day descends, it is time for a siesta in the shade, soothed by the hum of cicadas and the pungent scents of lemon and olive trees and herbs rising from the hot earth.

swedish

The main elements of Swedish rural style are simplicity, a sense of space and an understated elegance – all perfectly attuned to contemporary taste.

The formal elegance that typifies the Swedish look, known as Gustavian style, owes much to one man, King Gustav III. During the 1770s and 1780s, Gustav introduced to Sweden new decorating ideas from France and espoused in his palaces a form of Neoclassicism that was simpler and more austere than what had gone before. The elegance and restraint of Gustavian style filtered down through the aristocracy to the peasant classes, who interpreted the style in their own humble farmhouses, making use of the materials available to them.

Swedish country style is a tale of resourcefulness and adaptation. Even the poorest peasants adapted foreign fashions to Swedish conditions. Costly French pieces were recreated in cheap softwoods such as pine; fine tapestries and wall hangings were imitated by stencilled designs or wall paintings; and wooden mantelpieces were often decorated with *trompe l'oeil* marbling.

Above Tints of pale blue, muted grey and off-white create a gentle, luminous glow in this tranquil kitchen. Blue denim is an unusual choice for the elegant Gustavian chairs flanking the table.

Right A painted tin splashback enlivens a pantry corner.

Left The Georgian façade of this English farmhouse belonging to the furniture designer Lena Proudlock belies its Swedish country interior.

This page A large dresser, its panelled doors highlighted in gold leaf, is adorned with an array of blue and white china. The cotton runner and painted floorboards are typical of Swedish country interiors.

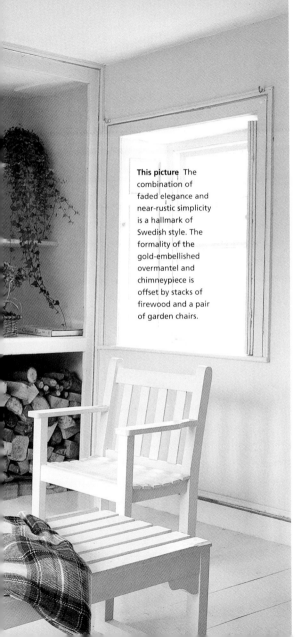

This picture The combination of faded elegance and near-rustic simplicity is a hallmark of Swedish style. The formality of the gold-embellished overmantel and chimneypiece is offset by stacks of firewood and a pair of garden chairs.

In a country where natural light is at a premium during the dark months of winter, walls were painted in pale, reflective colours to give the impression that rooms were suffused with light. Doors were left open to increase the feeling of spaciousness, while windows were curtained with the sheerest of muslins in order not to restrict daylight. Furniture and beds were upholstered in simple checks, stripes and florals. The overall effect is one of spare elegance and sophisticated simplicity.

To recreate the Swedish country look, paint your walls in delicate, luminous colours such as palest duck-egg green or ice blue, muted shell pink or soft pewter grey. Decorate walls with *trompe l'oeil* panelling, naive friezes of vines and flowers or simple, unfussy stencilled designs. Use rich, strong colours such as grass green or rust red on furniture or in woven and printed textiles.

Give careful consideration to the arrangement of furniture, displaying only a few chosen pieces in each room. Softly illuminate Swedish-style interiors with candlelight, and watch the pale colours glow in the lambent light.

Perhaps the enduring popularity of Swedish style is due to its effortless combination of elegant and utilitarian elements. The decorative approach is governed by a desire for symmetry and order, beauty and practicality, together with a deeply personal love of home.

Left Overlooking the lush Pennsylvania countryside, this pre-Revolutionary house is steeped in history.

Below Unexpected touches on the porch include crisp blue and white painted stripes and huge antique tin tubs for holding firewood.

Right The warm wooden panelling, old pewter plates and creamy-white upholstery capture the strength and simplicity of early American style.

early american

Strength, resourcefulness and sober elegance characterize the houses of the early New World settlers – a style that still lends itself to country living today.

American country style was forged by a cross-section of peoples who migrated to a land that was utterly strange to them. Early settlers endeavoured to create new homes in styles that were familiar to them, and in doing so applied building traditions from across Europe, adapting them to New World conditions. This led to the evolution of several distinctive early American architectural styles, each guided by a practical and modest aesthetic.

Pilgrim communities were blessed with a singularly abundant material that would determine the look of new homes across the land: wood. Early settlers were overwhelmed by the discovery of enormous forests filled with all manner of exotic trees, including wild cherry, hickory and cypress, to name just a few. These beautiful timbers were not only used to make shelters; they were also transformed into the exquisite furniture and objects that are now associated with early American style.

The north-eastern states, as far south as the Commonwealth of Virginia, were initially the most populated areas, colonized mainly by the English, and

the style that evolved here is known as Colonial. This sober and elegant style is characterized by dark wood panelling, simple furniture that owed much to English vernacular items, and a delicate palette of colours. Milk paint gave woodwork a soft sheen, and this decorative frugality was enhanced by plain, dyed linens and homespun cloth.

In New England, early settlers built dwellings that were closely related to the weatherboarded houses of south-east England. The interiors had scrubbed wooden floors, brightened with boldly coloured rag rugs. Furniture was a combination of pieces brought from the Old Country and newer items handcarved from indigenous woods.

Above and above right A traditional chequerboard design has been used to decorate the kitchen floorboards, but the blue and white paint adds a contemporary note and is a bold foil for the china.

Opposite A classic 18th-century sofa blends well with the simple lines of a limed cupboard.

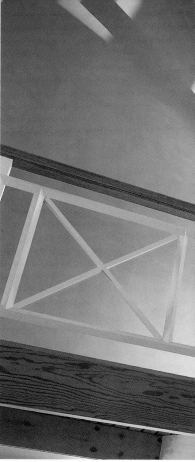

modern country

The easy country interior for a 21st-century home is spacious and pared down, but, as far as materials and integrity are concerned, it remains closely in touch with its rural roots.

Modern country style is much more than a passing fashion. Rather, it is a way of living that combines the warmth and honesty of the rural interiors of the past with a simplicity and practicality that is entirely contemporary. Space, light and natural materials are the essence of modern country.

Many old country houses are full of poky, low-ceilinged little rooms – rooms that could be warmed by coal and wood fires in winter. Windows were deliberately kept small; builders did not have the technology to create large expanses of glass and, besides, big windows would only allow chilly draughts to penetrate. However, modern developments such as central heating and good insulation have removed the need for those enclosed spaces. In these days of radiators, blinds and well-fitting windows, ceilings soar, walls are made of glass,

and bedrooms can be as large and airy as those in a Tuscan villa. Open space is an important element of the modern rural look. The quickest way to summon up a light, spacious feel in a small room is to paint walls, floors and ceilings white or cream and replace heavy curtains with simple blinds. More adventurous

Far left Architect Chris Cowper has turned a 200-year-old brick and flint barn into a practical, colourful home.

Left The wooden banisters and railings suggest the interior of a ship.

Below The upstairs sitting room offers ever-changing views of sea and marsh. Plain plank doors and window detail, white woodwork and blue-washed walls enhance the seaside feel.

alterations could include removing doors from their hinges and knocking down dividing walls to create more open space.

Natural materials are an essential ingredient of modern country interiors. The grain of wood, the strata of slate, the rounded forms of pebbles – all serve as constant reminders of the natural world, and all have an elemental quality that is deeply appealing to the eye and the touch. Choose stone or wooden floors – they will last for centuries and develop a

pleasing patina of age. Similarly, brick, wood and plaster walls all possess a tactile textural appeal.

Items of furniture need to be chosen carefully and sympathetically. The sturdy simplicity and grace of Shaker pieces, contemporary wicker or cane furniture, ancient chests and settles – all are well suited to a modern country interior.

Hardwearing, unpretentious fabrics such as calico and cotton and chunky utilitarian tableware will both strike the right note in a modern country scheme. Whatever you want to put in your home, pick the simplest and best things you can afford – they will be more likely to be well made and stand the test of time.

In a modern rural interior, the unique personality of the occupant should be allowed to shine through. There are, however, quintessential modern country elements that should be incorporated. For example, the warmth and beauty of wood brings us into close contact with the natural world and exerts a soothing, reassuring influence. Textural contrasts – a combination of smooth plaster and rough coir matting, or of cold stone and crisp cottons – are appealing to the senses. And, instead of subscribing to changing fashions, choose well-made, functional items that will improve with age and display them proudly, just as our ancestors would have done.

Above An artfully arranged group of pebbles frames a vase of fresh daisies.

Above left Small windows set into thick walls create a feeling of intimacy in a bedroom corner.

Opposite Ocean-blue walls, exposed beams and crisp white linen recall a calm seascape.

colour and surfaces

Opposite Subtle use of soft red on an architrave highlights a door set into a pine-panelled wall.

For hundreds of years, most of the colours in the paints and fabrics used in rural homes were made from pigments obtained from local minerals and vegetables. Since the pigments were derived from the earth, they were almost all 'earth' colours, the exact shade depending on the soil's mineral content. For instance, some clays coloured by iron oxide produced the cheap and durable pigment yellow ochre, while a greenish clay containing manganese and iron made *terre verte* (literally, green earth). Limewashes and milk paints were often coloured or tinted with a dash of locally derived pigment, creating beautiful, pale shades of yellow, buff, green and pink. To this day, we associate these subtle, harmonious tones with country living.

This picture In the dining room of an American Colonial home, bright red paint picks out the window frame, its surround and the wood-panelled dado. The simple country furniture, neutral wooden floor and creamy yellow wall do not fight for attention with the red; rather, they allow it to occupy centre stage.

red

Ranging from rusty orange-reds and deep purple-reds through to pale pinks and peaches, red has long been linked with rural homes, both inside and out.

Red pigments come from a variety of sources – animal, vegetable and mineral. Traditionally, country-dwellers had one source of red pigment that was always readily available: the earth.

Red paint was produced from iron deposits in the soil that were extracted and then mixed with chalk and water to make distemper, or with casein, obtained from cow's milk, and a small amount of lime to make milk paint. The resulting rusty-red shade is now inextricably linked

Right The front door of a Swedish house is painted a soft barn red.

with buildings in countryside settings. Since red paint was easy to obtain, many farmhouses and rural outbuildings, from Sweden to the USA, were painted in strong reds. But the shades and tones of red paint varied from region to region, ranging from a bright rust to a gingery brown to a ruddy purple, depending on the mineral content of the soil.

In the USA, bold rooster red is linked with the Colonial era, whereas warm

Above Cheerful red and white curtains make a dormer window into an eye-catching focal point.

Right Old wood panelling stained a rich terracotta and checked upholstery set the tone for a modern rustic look.

terracotta is more characteristic of the Mediterranean, and a strong pink shade is still common in East Anglia.

As the colour of these simple paints depended on the amount of pigment used and the amount of minerals in the pigment, every batch was almost unique, impossible to recreate exactly. This is most evident in the case of the red barns that are dotted across a vast swathe of American farmland, each one a slightly different shade of red from the next.

Vegetable sources were used to make dye to colour textiles, and madder, extracted from the madder plant, was the main source of red dye. However, country-dwellers would also have bought fabric at local stores or from travelling salesmen, and this material was often coloured with chemical dyes. This would explain the vivid scarlet patches, cut from red flannel petticoats, that occasionally appear in old patchwork quilts.

In modern country interiors, the earthiness of deep rust complements natural materials such as slate and stone, while browny reds bring out the warmth of mellow old wood. Red is an assertive colour, so take care when choosing red paints. What appears to be a countrified rust-red in the pot may be a fiery scarlet on the wall – a colour that is totally unsuitable for a country-style interior. When used on exterior surfaces, red paint produced from natural pigments fades gracefully, the sun gradually bleaching it to mellow terracotta or deep pink. Luckily, it is now possible to choose paints that convey a weathered, faded effect.

Vibrant reds should not be ruled out completely in an easy country interior. As long as it is used in an unsophisticated context, a bold splash of zingy tomato red or flaming crimson, for example, will inject warmth and vitality into the simplest and

Below Dull madder paint harmonizes with the traditional black and white chequered floor.

Above A mix of red and white evokes a rural feel, as in this Kentucky bedroom. The peg rail, dado rail and architrave are picked out in barn red, which looks fresh against the white walls. This crisp combination is echoed in the red and white quilts, the curtains and the valances. The red-painted floor pulls the decorative scheme together.

most understated interior. Red has a wonderful capacity to pull together diverse elements in a decorative scheme, particularly when it is used as part of the time-honoured country combination of red and white. Red and white gingham creates an aura of fresh and homely domestic charm yet possesses a bold simplicity that is entirely contemporary. Bright, shiny, fire-engine red enamelware in the French style is also completely in keeping with an easy country kitchen, and brightly coloured, loosely woven, Indian cottons patterned with contrasting checks will also contribute to an atmosphere of comfortable ease.

This page Deep Williamsburg blue is a good choice for the wooden panels and door of a Colonial interior in Connecticut. What might have been an overpowering colour is tempered by the white walls, the wooden floor and furniture, and the soft gleam of pewter plates on the mantelpiece.

blue

Although not widely available for use in interior decoration until the 18th century, restful blue tones captured the hearts of the Swedes, the Shakers and the early American settlers.

Although nature is full of blues, for many centuries there were only two sources of blue pigment: indigo and lapis lazuli. Ultramarine, made from powdered lapis lazuli, was a rare pigment that was too expensive to be used by anyone but the extremely wealthy. In contrast, the natural vegetable dye obtained from the indigo plant was cheap and plentiful, and was shipped into Europe from India in great quantities during the 18th century.

Above Blue and white can look elegant when complemented by stylish accessories.

Left Grey-tinged blue is a fittingly icy shade to show off a collection of skates.

However, as a pigment, indigo was not very permanent, so was unsuitable for making paint. It was widely used to dye cloth, but tended to fade dramatically.

It was not until the chance discovery, in the early 18th century, of Prussian blue, that an intense blue pigment became widely available. Soon, artificial ultramarine and cobalt blue were also being manufactured. By the mid-19th century, synthetic blue pigments were

Left Strong blue and white contrasts, often seen in seaside schemes, work well in any rural setting. In this fisherman's cottage converted into a holiday house, a rowing boat with decaying paintwork seems to be floating on a calm blue sea.

Below left A blue-grey washable paint gives this utilitarian kitchen table a touch of elegance that harmonizes with a set of creamy-white Gustavian chairs.

Below right Bright blue woodwork and white plaster make a shimmering contrast that maximizes the little light that enters a Mediterranean bathroom.

available from travelling salesmen, but they were expensive and not widely available. Since country-dwellers had little access to synthetic pigments, the blues used in their interiors were muted and subdued, with green or grey tones. There is little history of the use of bright electric blues in vernacular buildings and country interiors, and as a result, they are not often associated with country style. Different blue shades are associated with different country styles. Soft grey and greeny-blues dominate

the Swedish palette. The blue-green shade so typical of Swedish interiors was not created from synthetic blues, but was mixed from the earth pigment terra verte and the casein in milk to create a durable milk paint that covered wood panelling and furniture and did not rub off. Walls were covered with limewash or distemper, tinted in pale blue or grey. These cool Swedish blues bring a sense of light and space to an interior and harmonize well with off-white, pewter grey and strong terracotta hues.

A similar dull greeny-blue shade was adopted by the Shakers for staining woodwork in their meeting houses and retiring rooms. In one recipe recorded in a Shaker commonplace book, pulverized indigo was mixed with sulphuric acid and left to stand for two days. It was then

This page The sense of being at sea is strongly yet subtly felt everywhere in this converted barn. Daylight bounces off the curved chalky blue walls just as it does off water.

Far left Coolness and calm pervade the hallway of a Suffolk farmhouse. The effect derives from the combination of the natural earth tones of the brick floor and the soft blue of the flat-cut stair balustrade. The star quilt on the sofa was the starting point for the scheme.

Left Muted naturals and the soft blue of the checked cotton rug are paired on the landing, giving way to the crisper dark blue and white checked linen in the bedroom beyond.

Right In an old Texan farmhouse, sky blue meets corn yellow and earth brown in a colour combination that clearly has its roots in the surrounding countryside.

diluted with water and pearl ash was added until the desired colour was achieved. A paler sky blue, used for painting furniture and the insides of cupboards, was concocted from Prussian blue pigment and white lead. The Shakers rarely combined more than two colours in an interior. Blue was frequently teamed with white or a dark brick red to create a simple yet subtly elegant effect.

Blue panelling and woodwork is often associated with the American Colonial era. Williamsburg, in Colonial Virginia, even gave its name to the strong blue shade characteristic of Colonial interiors. This flat grey-blue works happily with other classic Colonial colours – rust red and straw yellow – and brings an air of understated dignity to simple country-style interiors.

Stronger splashes of blue can also introduce vibrancy to country interiors. A mixture of blue and white is a classic pairing that is especially well suited to rural-style kitchens. The colour combination first gained popularity in Europe in the 17th century, when cargoes of blue and white porcelain started to arrive from China. Europeans copied these exotic wares and established their own blue and white traditions: Delft from Holland, azulejo tiles from Portugal and English willow pattern. Wholesome blue gingham and bold blue and white pottery will create a crisp, clean effect in easy country kitchens without looking too fussy or excessively traditional.

green

Easy country greens should emulate the green hues that were traditionally made from earth and vegetable pigments.

Until the 20th century, few permanent green pigments were available in rural communities. The most common greens available to country-dwellers were those extracted from natural sources, such as

Above Adjacent rooms in a former barn on the coast are painted aqua green and blue.

Above left A green wash on panelling shows off the grain of the wood and harmonizes with the antique table.

Left Green tones in a garland of oak leaves and acorns above a doorway on a pale-green wall recall early green pigments.

Opposite Light falling on an undulating aqua-toned wall evokes a sense of the sea.

copper oxide and the earth. Terre verte, a blue-green colourwash made from green clay, was the most common form of green paint and appeared in country interiors across northern Europe and America. It was often used to make a milk paint for wooden panelling or to colour limewash for plastered walls.

Terre verte was frequently mixed with white to produce a range of beautiful soft greyish-greens. These were popular colours for decorating country interiors in both Europe and America during the 17th century. The soft, muted tones create an impression of cool classic elegance, and work equally well today in contemporary country-style interiors, especially when they are combined with other natural colours such as creams, ochres and browns.

In some Mediterranean countries, a bright aquamarine derived from copper carbonate, a by-product of copper mining, was added to limewashes and used to paint exterior wood such as shutters and doors. Like the saturated blue characteristic of Mediterranean decoration, this chalky green appears bright in sunlight but acquires a quiet intensity in the shade. When contrasted with expanses of dazzling white, it becomes a vibrant sea-green.

In the 19th century, the development of chemical dyes led to the creation of a palette of vivid, showy greens that were positively dazzling in comparison with the subtle, light greens created from natural pigments and vegetable dyes. However, by the late 19th century, the members of the Arts and Crafts

movement, inspired by William Morris, spearheaded a return to the use of natural vegetable dyes, which created muted, sober, even sludgy, green hues.

Green's complementary colour is red – in other words, green and red are direct opposites on the colour wheel. The two colours are contrasting yet often make a successful alliance. Cool greeny-grey hues work particularly well with warmer shades such as gingery red or

Left In a old Texan farmhouse where German settlers stencilled borders on walls and ceilings, shades of green are seen in every room.

Above The boarded walls in this room are painted a rich bluish-green, with a more muted tone used in the floral border.

rich terracotta – a combination of colours that can be seen in many interiors of the American Colonial period.

In easy country interiors, subdued shades of green provide an understated backdrop for cool white linen, simple painted furniture and objects made from pale metals such as silver and pewter. In a bedroom or bathroom, such shades instill a tranquil atmosphere. Green is an ideal colour for stencilling and freehand

decorative painting – much of which traditionally featured botanical motifs.

Reminiscent of foliage and freshness, splashes of green can introduce a sense of the natural world into a room. A painted or stencilled garland of leaves on a plastered wall, a leaf-green cushion, an olive-toned Provençal glazed bowl, and, of course, armfuls of greenery from the garden can all be used to great effect to bring in a feeling of the outdoors.

Above The living-room walls have a simple band of yellow stencilling echoed in the narrow garland on the cream ceiling.

Left This garden room in the south of France – its terracotta fireplace illuminated by the sun's last rays – is the perfect place for alfresco dining.

Opposite The rough terracotta plaster of the mantel shows an underlying green-blue finish which is picked up by the bleached wooden moulding above.

Below The mixture of rich ochre tones and intense green foliage is typical of the Mediterranean colour palette.

yellow and orange

The natural pigments of yellow ochre and raw sienna have been used since ancient times to create the soft golden yellows, terracottas and ambers reminiscent of sun-filled rural interiors.

In country interiors, the only yellow that plays an important role is the warm, honeyed yellow-orange shade derived from yellow ochre. Cool yellow and vibrant tangerine do not have a long decorating history and, accordingly, are not characteristic of country interiors. Warm rich yellows and mellow oranges, on the other hand, have been used in country dwellings for thousands of years. Yellow and orange paint was produced

Left The natural timber in this Kentucky log cabin is complemented by a rich buttery yellow.

Right Barn red and yellow are a classic combination for easy country style. Here, in a Kentucky log cabin, the warm red of the stairs harmonizes with the yellow of the painted panelling.

Below Yellow lights up a landing under the eaves of a house in southern France.

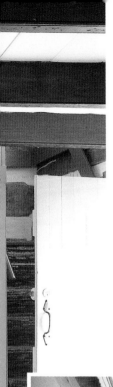

from the natural pigments – ochre and raw sienna – that occur in clays and sands in many regions of the world. These pigments have always been cheap and easy to obtain, so earthy yellow and warm orange shades have a long history in both interior and exterior house painting. Warm creamy yellow hues or muted orange and terracotta tones are equally at home in an old Swedish farmhouse, an English country cottage, a Shaker schoolroom and a Provençal villa.

Ochre was the only yellow that was commercially available as a pigment until as late as 1820, when chrome yellow burst upon the scene, giving rise to the vibrant, dazzling yellows of the Empire period. Somehow these acidic artificial yellows are more suited to silks and taffetas than cottons and linens, and a country palette is more likely to favour the soft hues of straw and sand than brassy sulphuric yellows.

Soft golden yellow brings mellow warmth to any interior. Yellow ochre was responsible for the rich eggnog shade that is synonymous with the American Colonial period as well as the earthy orange and terracotta so widely used in Italy and Provence. Combined with white pigments, ochre was used in milk paints to create a homely, buttery colour or pale straw tone for interior walls or woodwork. In Scandinavia, pale creamy yellows are used on walls to maximize the effect of daylight while bringing warmth to an interior.

The Shakers also included yellow in their colour palette and were highly inventive in the number of sources they discovered for their yellow dyes. These included young fustic (from the Venetian sumac tree), barberry bush, peach leaves,

sugar of lead, saffron and onion skins. Yellow was generally used as a stain for wood rather than as a paint. Shaker furniture is frequently stained yellow. Floors of dwelling houses and shops were finished with yellowish-red stains.

In common with many other Shaker techniques, wood staining fits in well with the ethos of easy country style. It introduces subtle colour without obscuring the natural grain and texture of the wood, and a yellowish stain will enhance the wood's natural colour.

In a north-facing room, a warm wash of yellow will create the illusion of sun-warmed walls. An orangey-ochre wash will also impart a gentle warmth to the exterior of houses. The right yellow will work just as well in cool northern light as in the south. The Swedes often used a pale ochre shade on their country manor houses, offset by white window surrounds, and this colour combination was also imitated by the peasant classes.

Above Original iron door furniture in a Colonial house in Maine looks smart against distressed painted woodwork.

Above left Straw-yellow walls brought a sense of sunshine into otherwise dark Colonial farmhouses. The effect would have been enhanced after nightfall by the use of mirror-backed candle sconces.

Left Traditionally, the Shaker peg rail was used to hang up clothes, baskets, chairs and other household items.

Yellow's reaction to other colours can be surprising. Pale straw or golden yellow works well with barn red. With blue it is important to match the two colours tonally, so cobalt blue and faded ochre or duck-egg and straw are happy together, but mix two different intensities and you will upset the delicate balance. When yellow and green are paired, the most successful hues for a country interior are chalky aquamarines and ochres rather than zingy modern lemons and limes.

Above An openfronted cupboard has been painted acid yellow, a colour that became popular in the first quarter of the 19th century with the advent of chrome yellow pigment. The colour adds zest to what would otherwise be a very utilitarian piece of furniture.

Above and opposite A mix of creams and whites adds a fresh feel to a Provençal attic. The coolness of the pebble-inlaid concrete floor is echoed in the white-painted timber ceiling, while cream-coloured, natural-linen bedding looks crisply enticing.

Right The white theme is continued in an elaborately carved dresser.

white and cream

Rather than stark clinical whites, choose chalky whites, creamy whites, milky whites and sunbleached whites to bring a sense of restful simplicity to an easy country interior.

Dazzling titanium white – not a country colour – was first produced in the 1920s. Before that, people decorated their houses using a whole palette of natural white and cream shades, and these are the hues that still look best in a rural setting. We only have to look outside to understand why.

In nature, every white flower is a different shade of white. Even snow is not pure white. It is grey, blue, ochre, pink – subtly tinted by the fall of sun and shadow.

Chalky, soft whites and creams are typical of country interiors and exteriors. Limewash, perhaps the oldest paint in the world, dates back thousands of years. It was used by country-dwellers the world over as part of an annual

spring-clean, protecting buildings inside and out, and repairing the ravages caused by winter rain and snow. After several coats, limewash dries to a clean, opaque white that is bright and luminous in sunlight and matt and chalky in the shade. In its function as a paint, limewash exhibits natural properties that, until the 20th century, could not be bettered. The lime in the wash disinfects, cleanses and allows moisture to evaporate, keeping walls free of bacteria, damp and insects.

In Swedish houses, white-painted walls and furniture often, on closer inspection, turn out to be a drab cream or a pale shade of grey. The Swedes devised chalky, off-white limewashes and distempers that softened the harsh, cold light of the north. They also made use of texture: architectural detailing would be painted a slightly different shade of grey, and wood was not painted over entirely, but limewashed, allowing the grain to show through.

The symbolic purity of white was highly esteemed by the Shakers, who decreed that the exteriors of meeting houses alone could be painted white, to distinguish them from houses, barns and workrooms. In their interiors, the Shakers frequently combined clean white walls with dark, sombre green, strong blue or deep red woodwork, creating an orderly, spacious and simple effect. In an easy country interior, white and cream can be used to produce a

Above left In days gone by, fresh white paint would show that the annual disinfecting coat of limewash had been applied. The need for this has passed, but white still gives a sense of freshness and cleanliness. In this room, ice white has been applied to every possible wood surface so that they all blend together.

Above right Storage cupboards in a wide hallway have been painted, along with the walls, in pure white. The cupboard doors with their ventilation holes are reminiscent of old food safes.

Top left Antique wire kitchen utensils create a decorative effect against the whitewashed walls of a Texan log cabin.

Top right Old half-timbering has been painted a uniform fresh white for the easy country look.

Opposite In a large hallway, a sense of light and space has been created by the use of creamy white paint on all the woodwork. The effect is softened by the rush matting on the floor.

Left Demonstrating that white need not be cold and clinical, shades of white and very pale blues and greys blend happily in a Scandinavian-style kitchen.

Right In this old Pennsylvania farm dwelling, the formal overmantel contrasts with the plastered and whitewashed rustic fireplace.

delicate, romantic effect or a sense of timeless simplicity. The gentle whites that predominate in Scandinavian regions will introduce a soft, restrained elegance, while purer, cleaner whites provide the perfect background for the functional grace and elegant lines of Shaker furniture.

The bleached, dazzling white that is traditionally associated with the Mediterranean region can be teamed with contrasting shades of strong, saturated blue, vibrant aquamarine or dusty terracotta to create a bold contemporary look that is reminiscent of the Mediterranean landscape.

The use of white in many minimal modern interiors means that the colour has become associated with a clinical, hospital-like austerity. If it is used carefully, however, white can be totally compatible with easy country style, and to consider it as cold and severe is to miss the point. There are few sensual pleasures to equal that of slipping between crisp, white linen sheets or of putting on a clean white cotton shirt that has been dried in the hot sun. In addition, white brings a simple luxury to household items such as nubbly cotton towels, bone-handled cutlery, linen napkins and chunky white crockery.

floors

A floor covering sets the tone for an easy country interior. There is a wide array of possibilities to choose from, including wood, stone, terracotta, natural fibres and rough concrete.

Right A multi-coloured rag rug covers the barn-red stairs of an old log cabin. This is an innovative touch. Rag rugs were not traditionally used on staircases.

Opposite The wide floorboards in a cosy country parlour have been painted in a traditional black and white chequerboard pattern. The effect is to transform the room into a rather grand-looking space.

The earliest country houses had floors made from pounded or stamped earth. The hard floors that replaced them were made from many different materials, depending on what was locally available. Terracotta tiles were favoured in the Spanish *finca* or Provençal *mas*, while in densely forested Scandinavia and America, wooden floors were most common. In England, rough-hewn flagstones were found in many cottages. These attractive natural materials are all very durable and, with the passage of time, develop a pleasing patina of age.

Historically, another important factor in the choice of floor materials was the climate. In the Mediterranean region, cool stone, glazed ceramic tiles and terracotta were favoured, while in cooler climates, hard floors such as wood or stone were covered with handmade matting or rugs to provide a modicum of comfort and warmth underfoot. The conveniences of modern living such as central heating and effective insulation mean that nowadays climate tends to be less of a consideration when choosing country-style floor coverings. Terracotta tiles can evoke the impression of the sunny Mediterranean in a New York City apartment, while scrubbed Swedish-style floors can grace a London townhouse.

If your house has retained its original floorboards, it is well worth removing any carpets that have been laid on top and having the boards restored, even if you have to replace some of them – the rich, mellow colouring and rustic effect of old oak or pine cannot be imitated. The perfect smoothness of a new wood floor has its own appeal, and will bring a sense of spaciousness and purity to any interior. In rural parts of northern Europe and Scandinavia there is a long tradition of painting wooden floors. Farmers and peasants painted the floors in their humble farmhouses in imitation of the expensive tiled and parquet floors of the aristocracy. Painted floors inject instant colour into a room and the decorative

possibilities are huge. Wooden floors do not require much upkeep – the patina of wear and tear on a painted or waxed wood floor merely enhances its charms.

Other hard floor coverings include brick and terracotta tiles. Both are made from clay, and they possess a mellow warmth that is immediately evocative of comfortable, homely country interiors. Like wooden floors, brick and terracotta develop a pleasing patina of age.

Another durable and cheap material, concrete, is an innovative flooring choice that can undergo a total transformation when dressed up. To create a rustic impression, roughly finished concrete floors can be tinted in earth colours or even inset with tiles, pebbles, and other decorative items.

For warmer, more yielding flooring with a country feel, choose natural fibres such as jute, sisal, seagrass, coir or rush matting. These durable materials have been used as country-floor coverings for

centuries – rush matting, for example, dates back to medieval times. They add a rustic simplicity to an interior, and their rough, nubbly texture is pleasantly tactile underfoot. Braided, hooked and rag rugs also evoke the homespun comfort of an authentic rural interior. Loom-woven mats were part of the Shaker tradition. Colours were strictly regulated and confined to two or three per mat, but, even within these constraints, their makers still managed to produce objects of beauty. Woven cotton or flax rugs were common in Swedish country homes, where they took the form of long runners that were folded in on themselves to turn a corner. In modern country interiors, runners are very decorative and practical, too, since they can easily be taken up and washed. The timeless, elemental quality of these raw materials used as floor coverings is entirely in tune with the new, pared-down approach to country living.

Above left A subtly coloured flatweave rug is well suited to easy country style.

Above centre Painting a pattern on a wooden floor gives the floor a simple charm.

Above right Small blue and cream ceramic tiles are just the right scale for a country bathroom.

Opposite Utilitarian concrete is given an easy country twist with the unexpected addition of pigment and a pebble design.

walls

Easy country walls incorporate authentic limewash and milk paint, traditional stencilling, freehand decoration, and plenty of plain or painted woodwork.

In many country buildings, walls act as expressive elements. They often have an organic quality – the natural materials they are made from relate them to the landscape they inhabit. Massive log walls are redolent of warmth and safety; weatherboarding evokes a comforting sense of protection against the elements; and slabs of rough-hewn stone speak of strength and security.

Wooden walls are sensual. They invite us to breathe in, inhaling the aromatic scents of resin, wax or linseed. In old country houses, wooden walls took the form of horizontal or vertical planking, panelling or tongue-and-groove. In modern houses, unpainted wooden cladding has a sensuous, tactile appeal. However, painted wooden walls are more historically authentic if the aim is to create a country atmosphere.

In rural areas, paint for woodwork was made from powdered pigment, casein from buttermilk and a little lime. The result was milk paint, which gave an attractive, durable sheen to the surface of the wood. Milk paint was used on woodwork in Europe and Scandinavia

Top Hand-hewn logs alternating with thick plaster are typical of the inside of log cabins and farmhouses.

Above left Rough logs painted white are classics of the easy country style.

Above right Taking advantage of large stocks of indigenous timber growing in the surrounding countryside, Colonial Americans were able to make a feature of wooden panelling in their homes.

Opposite Rows of overlapping timber shingles are used to weatherproof an exterior wall. The blue milk paint of the door and steps makes a brilliant contrast with the natural wood.

from the 17th century. Painted wooden walls were common in rural Scandinavian homes, where strong colours such as rust red and apple green were used to inject vitality into rooms that were unavoidably dark in winter. However, milk paint is most closely associated with American Colonial houses of the 18th century, where wooden walls were painted in rich shades of green, blue and red.

In Colonial America, paintmakers or 'color men' travelled around selling pigments that could be mixed with local ingredients to make milk paint. The resulting paint was thicker and more paste-like than thin modern paints. The paint was rubbed hard into the grain of the wood and one coat of paint would last virtually a lifetime. It is difficult to recreate this lustrous, textured effect with modern paints. Perhaps the effect of staining is closer than that of modern

painting, since it allows the grain of the wood to show through. If wooden walls are to be left unpainted, there is a choice of finishes, depending on the type of wood. Matt varnish is most suitable for pine, while open-grained hardwoods such as oak prefer linseed oil.

Timber panelling was originally a feature seen only in grander European homes, but, owing to the abundance of wood in the New World, panelling became a decorative trend in modest homes in Colonial America. In northern Europe, entire rooms were panelled; by contrast, in the New World, panelling usually featured on fireplace walls or was extended only up to dado height. Panelling has a wonderful historical feel to it and is particularly attractive when painted with milk paint in authentic American Colonial colours, such as Williamsburg blue or rusty ox-blood red.

Plaster is another wall covering that was traditionally applied for insulation

Left Modern bleached wooden planking – rather nautical in feel – lines the walls of a seaside home.

Below left Based on old fishermen's dwellings, the walls of this one-room cottage are made of adobe and wood. The designer has embedded locally grown bamboo in the adobe for a decorative touch.

Opposite The wall's horizontal planks, with their visible nail heads, have real country charm. The ravages of time and weather have given the wood a gentle, distressed finish.

but which is now seen as beautiful in its own right. Plasterers of the past worked hard to achieve a perfectly smooth finish, but now an uneven, slightly textured wall is more desirable in country-style homes. In humble rural dwellings, limewash was used on plastered walls up until the mid-19th century, when whitewash began to replace it. Whitewash is more permanent than limewash and does not rub off, but also dries to a chalky finish. Whitewash, too, can be coloured by powdered pigments. To achieve a similar effect in modern homes, choose specialist paints that emulate the effect of old-style limewashes or distempers.

Freehand painting and stencilling were originally a form of decoration favoured by the poorer classes of society. In Sweden, peasants employed paint to imitate expensive materials such as marble. Some of the people who painted faux marble had never seen the real thing and their efforts fall wide of the mark but possess a naive charm of their own. Stencilling dates back to the Middle Ages, when it was used to decorate the interior of churches. In the 19th century it became a cheaper alternative to wallpaper. In modern times, these crafts are appreciated in their own right. Their naivety is better suited to an easy country home than manufactured wallpaper designs would be, and even the simplest painted adornment will introduce a touch of originality to a room.

furnishings

Despite their varied origins, country furnishings frequently share an elegant simplicity, born of the fact that they were first and foremost utilitarian objects. As a result, rustic furniture from different periods and countries can coexist harmoniously. Country furnishings need not all be antique. Modern items can be at home in an easy country interior, as long as they possess a few essential features. They should be made from natural materials and possess a simplicity of line and a sturdy, practical grace. Above all, easy country furnishings should not be hard-edged, pristine and spotless, but tactile, welcoming and comfortable.

tables

Styles of country table range from large, long kitchen tables for eating and preparing food to small, foldaway space-saving designs, but the emphasis remains firmly on the practical.

In medieval times, many country people ate, slept and worked in a single-room dwelling, and the earliest country tables were rudimentary affairs: boards resting on trestles that were cleared away at the end of a meal. It was not until the 16th century that tables assumed their familiar four-legged form. Even then, in rural communities in Europe and, later, among the log-cabin pioneers of the New World, the logistics of one-room living meant that the table was often a dispensable item.

Long refectory-style tables date from the late 16th century. More prosperous rural dwellers, such as farmers, occupied larger houses, and the centrepiece of the kitchen was always a large, long table. They have been an essential element of country kitchens all over the world ever since.

The need to save space in small country dwellings gave rise to many ingenious table designs. Monks' benches had backs that lifted up onto the arms to form a table. The drop-leaf table, a design that is still common today, was popular in

Above A mahogany table with a single drawer plays a useful role in a French country kitchen.

Right A low table has been covered by a cheerful blue and white cloth in a contemporary interpretation of country style.

Far right Small wooden tables were often made from wood grown on the property. Now they have become very collectable.

Opposite A sturdy two-drawer table has the strength and solidity to hold its own against the massive rough timber walls of this early Colonial dwelling. A table like this would have been the focal point of family life in the country.

Left and above Very popular in Sweden, the drop-leaf table is hugely practical. This one can seat eight people but folds up to occupy the narrowest of spaces and can be placed out of the way against a wall.

Opposite, above An unassuming country table on a wooden porch provides a extra work surface.

Swedish homes. With side leaves and legs that swing out to support them, they convert from an narrow side table to a dining table that could seat eight comfortably.

Country-dwellers made their furniture from the materials that were to hand. Often the legs, stretchers and tops of tables were constructed from different woods – the legs were carved from hardwoods for strength while the tabletop was made from thicker and less expensive softwood planks. Such tables might be painted to hide the fact that they were made from different woods. Sometimes they were finished in a wood colour such as mahogany, but kitchen tables were usually left untreated, so they could be scoured and scrubbed.

Small side tables first appeared in the 17th century in the dining rooms of the aristocracy and gentry, but their usefulness meant that they soon filtered down to the peasantry and began to appear in country dwellings. These little tables, often with a small drawer, played a useful and versatile role in every room. Sometimes they were used as occasional desks or work tables. The Shakers produced large numbers of small work tables, each with a drawer for storing sewing or knitting materials.

Right Foldaway tables were space-savers in rural homes where all the family activities took place in one room. Today they can be used to inject a touch of country style.

Far right Occasional tables such as this 'demi-lune' were generally regarded as a luxury, but this simply constructed example has a place in a country interior.

chairs and benches

Country chairs and benches are wonderful examples of rural resourcefulness. They were made using simple handmade tools, natural materials and traditional skills handed down from generation to generation.

Basic, sometimes rough-hewn, country chairs frequently have a far greater appeal than a sophisticated classical chair. Their simplicity of form and their patina of age and usage represent the essence of easy country style.

When constructing a chair, country craftsmen chose their wood with care. They selected different woods for

Right A sturdy little chair with a woven rush seat is a country classic that can be seen the world over. It is equally at home in a bedroom or at a dining table or desk.

Below left Its backrest painted to tone with the ochre and blue palette, an old ladderback chair with woven seat has been given a touch of modern style.

Opposite The rocker is an archetypal country chair. This hand-carved example with woven seat and back stands on a shady porch.

Opposite, inset A beautiful French chair in chestnut with a woven seat is a variation on the simpler chair seen on the right. Its welcoming wooden arms and broad seat make it a desirable collector's item.

different objects – in Britain, oak was often used for furniture on account of its strength and durability. Wood was cut along the grain to retain maximum flexibility, and was then shaped by hand or by simple lathe. The wood for curved sections was steamed before being bent into shape while it was still malleable. Chairs were held together with whittled pegs and wedges.

Country chairs are available in a rich diversity of styles – different regions had their own distinct styles and traditions. However, some shapes and styles will always be associated with country living. The graceful ladderback chair is one

Above A sturdy garden chair looks quite at home in a country interior.

Above right In a new version of an old bench, the clean, simple lines of rustic furniture have been kept, but comfort has been added in the shape of deep upholstery and a reclining backrest.

Opposite In an early panelled room in a house in Connecticut, an English elm bench introduces a sense of resourcefulness and solidity. Using a bench like this instead of the more obvious chairs and sofa can imprint a strong country feel on a room.

such example – it has become a country classic in both Europe and America. Ladderbacks have three or four curved slats across the back. Traditionally, the seats were made from whatever local material was available – rushes by the river, rawhide in cowherding country and fisherman's rope by the coast. The most sophisticated examples of ladderback chairs were those made by the Shakers. These pieces were very sturdy yet light enough to be hung from a peg rail, and the seats were woven from hand-knitted fabric tapes. Ladderback chairs spread as far as Sweden during the 18th century. Many Swedish examples were painted and they frequently had padded seats upholstered in simple cottons.

The Windsor chair – characterized by its distinctive spokes set in a bowed frame and its sturdy saddle seat – is another rural classic. Originally an English style, it was adopted by the American colonists, and fine old examples can be found on both sides of the Atlantic. Both ladderback and Windsor chairs are still in production today, and their comfort and simplicity make them ideal for modern country interiors.

It may be something of a cliché, but the rocking chair on the porch appears to many people to sum up the unhurried pace of country living. Rocking chairs have always enjoyed greater popularity in America than Europe, perhaps due to the fact that there was usually one on every porch. Until the 20th century they were primarily regarded as chairs for the elderly, although the Shakers saw them as essential items and placed one in every retiring room.

Benches and settles are satisfyingly versatile pieces of furniture that are thought to have evolved from storage chests. Settles were originally built into the rooms in which they were needed, but by the end of the 16th century, freestanding pieces began to make their appearance. Benches and settles were truly multifunctional – the seat of the bench or settle covered a useful storage space for bedding or chamber pots. The monks' bench had a hinged back that lifted up to convert into a table. Some settles even had cupboards set into the back of them for the storage of food.

This page A modern four-poster with simple lines retains the feel of a simply constructed rustic bed. The loosely slung canopy of blue and white striped canvas is purely for dramatic effect.

beds

As preoccupations with keeping warm at night were replaced by concern for bedroom hygiene and cleanliness, country-bed designs changed accordingly.

In early country dwellings around the world, beds, like tables, did not occupy permanent positions. They often took the form of straw-filled mattresses laid out at night in the main room of the house so that sleepers could take advantage of the warmth emitted from the dying embers of the fire.

Historically, the design of country beds reveals a constant preoccupation with one thing – keeping warm. In cooler parts of the world such as Scandinavia or northern Europe, beds were sometimes built into recesses in the walls of a house that resembled cubbyholes; they were concealed behind doors richly painted with naive but colourful decorative motifs. Four-poster beds represented another attempt to keep warm in bed and were originally draped with thick, padded curtains to exclude draughts.

For many people living in the country, a bedstead was their most valuable possession. In central Europe, a wooden bed was often presented as a gift to a married couple and was intended to last them all their life before becoming an heirloom for future generations. Laden with symbolic value, these beds might be elaborately painted or carved with flowers and foliage or religious pictures. Children slept in the same room as their parents, usually in small trundle beds that could be tucked away beneath a larger bed during the daytime. Many children's beds were decorated with decorative carving or stencilling. The American pioneers constructed wooden bedsteads that could be easily taken apart and stored in the back of a covered wagon. When the pioneers finally settled in a homestead, the beds were slotted together again and covered with pallets stuffed with fresh, dry straw. Finally, thick, downy featherbeds were placed on top, covered by heavy quilts.

Early bed frames were made of wood and metal. During the 19th century, metal bedsteads were seen as a cheap and hygienic option, and so became a common sight in country bedrooms and servants' quarters. Traditional brass and iron bedsteads can often be found in junk shops or at antiques markets, but many are small by modern standards. Fortunately, reproduction models in more generous sizes are widely available. If you are lucky enough to find an unpainted brass bed, treasure it, for the metal will have acquired a pleasing patina of age. More frequently, metal bedsteads are painted black, but they can be transformed by a few coats of paint.

The ingenious Swedes devised space-saving extendable beds. When the beds were not in use, the bedhead and foot could be pushed together to halve the length of the bed – particularly useful in small country dwellings. In Sweden and France, more prosperous country-dwellers with some pretensions to style might have possessed a daybed. These elegant, three-sided beds were designed for versatility – they were used as sofas in the day then slept on at night.

When plucking poultry, country-women saved up the feathers and used them to make featherbeds, which must have seemed luxuriously soft to people used to sleeping on hard, scratchy straw-filled pallets. Feather mattresses were tremendously warm and yielding, rather like enormous, plump pillows, and were still in use in some country houses until quite recently. Most mattresses were supported on wooden slats laid across the bed frame, while other beds used rope threaded from side to side. This type of mattress support gave rise to the expression 'sleep tight', since it was possible to tighten the ropes to prevent the mattress from sagging.

Solid divan beds, which appeared in the 1950s, are neither attractive nor practical for a country bedroom. Dust collects beneath them and they are bulky, heavy and awkward to move around. Modern wooden beds with carved legs, headboards and footboards

Above Exuding an air of quiet elegance, this classic Colonial-style bed is one of a pair. If you cannot buy the real thing, copies of this type of design abound.

Right Lengths of stout rope threaded from side to side of the frame support the mattress in this American rope bed. Its elaborate finials recall a four-poster.

This page Lack of adornment was a distinctive feature of interiors in early American frontier towns, where life was harsh. This wooden headboard has a reassuringly simple shape and is unencumbered by fussy pillows or bedspreads.

Inset A more recent wooden headboard boasts machine-turned barley-twist posts and elaborate pierced carving. The bold red and white stripes of the quilt add a country touch.

Left Day beds conjure up an image of people with more time to spare than the average country-dweller, but a well-chosen design still has a place in an easy country interior. This metal day bed strewn with striped ticking cushions does not look at odds with its surroundings. Where space is at a premium, as in this tiny cottage, dual-purpose furniture can be both practical and stylish.

Opposite, below left
Were it not for its coat of washed-out apple-green paint, its cushions in simple country cottons, and its faded floral print bedcover, this pared-down version of the classic French *lit bateau* might have been too grand for its rustic timber-boarded home.

Opposite, below right Making good use of space and keeping warm were prime concerns in traditional country interiors. Here, a cosy bed has been built under the eaves, where little else would fit and where warm air would accumulate. The chequered quilts contribute to the bed's rustic appeal.

Right A spool bed, so called because the turned wood looks like spools of cotton placed end to end, is a classic 19th-century American country bed. Crisp blue and white linen and an antique quilt provide the perfect finishing touches.

and even posts can easily be found and are much more suited to an easy country bedroom. The Shakers constructed their wooden bedsteads on wooden rollers so that they could easily be moved out of the way to allow for cleaning.

Simple wood and metal four-posters are also widely available today, but to hang curtains around them looks merely like historical pastiche. Instead, why not sling a simple length of muslin casually over the top rail, fabricate a tabard from striped ticking and loop it across the top and behind the headboard, or simply leave the bed unadorned?

Nowadays, most of our houses have central heating, and improved insulation means that we have fewer icy draughts to contend with than was the case in

the past. Refreshing sleep is essential to maintain the fast, busy pace of modern life, so being self-indulgent when it comes to beds is completely justified. A mattress is one item that will not improve with age, so it is worth spending as much as you possibly can on a well-made, good-quality model. Even if you inherit or buy an antique bed, it is wise to invest in a new mattress to ensure a restful night's sleep. The same is true of pillows. A single, firm, good-quality pillow should ensure a comfortable and restorative night's rest. A mound of flouncy bolsters, lace-trimmed pillows and puffy eiderdowns is completely at odds with the simple spirit of easy country and, besides, they will only end up on the floor every night.

storage

For the easy country look, use well-made shelves and dressers to display only those objects that deserve to be displayed, and stow away the practical necessities of life in unfussy cupboards, chests and boxes.

Built-in cupboards were the earliest form of country storage. They were set into the thickness of the wall with a wooden door attached. Many were lockable and were used primarily to store foodstuffs, especially expensive bought items such as tea, spices and sugar, which they kept safe and dry, well-protected from marauding insects and vermin and away from the dirt and damp of the earth floor. Some early cupboards were even built into other pieces of furniture, such as the backs or seats of settles. Others were built into wall recesses, such as the medieval 'aumbry', a simple cupboard

This page, above left An old country cupboard, its colour now faded, displays a collection of pots.

This page, above right A utilitarian cupboard has been built into a chimney breast in a kitchen.

This page, below left Evolving from side tables, dressers such as this early English oak example made an attractive solution to everyday storage problems.

This page, below right A Colonial American cupboard is modelled on the furniture left behind by the settlers in the old country.

Opposite, above A sophisticated version of a built-in kitchen cupboard, this piece resembles a dresser.

Opposite, below left The simple detailing of these modern cupboards is in easy country style.

Opposite, below right An early freestanding kitchen storage cupboard has been set on high tapered legs to stave off hungry mice.

Opposite
Bookshelves built from floor to ceiling and above a sofa provide space-saving storage for a library. The scalloped ceiling moulding across the front of the shelving is extended across the window to add a feeling of unity.

set into the thickness of the wall that evolved into the classic French armoire.

Perhaps the archetypal piece of rural furniture is the dresser. Dressers evolved from side tables, some of which were fitted with drawers beneath the table top. When this simple piece was paired with a row of shelves set on top of it, the dresser was born. Both practical and decorative, it provided storage and display space at the same time. Dressers differed from area to area and country to country, and a number of distinctive styles developed. Some had a 'pot board' – a wide shelf beneath the drawers. Others had a lower section composed entirely of cupboards. Dressers could be built in or freestanding, painted or plain – there were numerous variations.

Today, a dresser offers ample storage space for an abundance of items, as well as providing valuable surfaces for display. Blue and white china looks wonderful against dark wood; Williamsburg blue

Above left In a country larder, open wooden shelves hold a collection of pots and baskets whose toning colours make an eye-catching display. Larders such as this one would originally have had a stone floor and marble shelves to keep food cool.

Right Deep, built-in cupboards with unfussy doors give maximum storage and leave a room looking uncluttered.

Above centre An antique plate rack provides useful extra kitchen storage and looks stylish in a country interior. You could hang one in its more usual position – over the kitchen sink.

Above right This set of bookshelves incorporates a very simple moulding that would be in keeping with a country interior.

Above left This unusual hanging shelf made from twigs is home to an eclectic collection of treasured items. The earth colours of the objects and the natural twigs would make a talking point in any rural interior.

Left and opposite, below We need more storage than our rural forebears required and we want things to look good too, so, when you are planning storage, always think about the quantity and size of what needs to be stored.

These blue-painted shelves are both practical and stylish.

Above Fine wire mesh was commonly used in place of solid cupboard doors, so that stored items were on view. Today, it offers an attractive rustic alternative to wooden panels. Here a collection of antique tablecloths and kitchen linen is on display behind a chicken-wire mesh.

Opposite, above An old dresser with a spoon rack has been perfectly designed for its purpose.

is the perfect backdrop to American creamware; and spongeware ideally complements mellowed pine.

Freestanding storage also included large wardrobes, blanket boxes, chests of drawers and chests. Wardrobes were most common in Scandinavia, central Europe and France. Many were painted with scrolling foliage and other motifs taken from nature. In France, the armoire, a large wardrobe-like structure often decorated with elaborate carving, was used to hold food or clothes.

Every American Colonial household possessed at least one sturdy wooden chest that had been used to store the family's few treasured possessions during the long transatlantic voyage. Once it had reached its destination, this versatile item was used for storing bedlinen, quilts, personal belongings and clothes. It could also be pressed into service as a spare seat or table when required. Country chests were produced in huge quantities across Europe and America, for they did not need much wood or a great deal of skill on the part of the woodworker. Well-preserved examples are quite easy to find at flea markets and in antiques shops, and will prove just as useful in a modern country-style home.

Wall-mounted shelves were typical of country kitchens, where they were intended to store items that were used and washed daily, such as plates, mugs, wooden spoons and scoops and cooking

pots. In modern kitchens, open shelves are much more attractive than serried ranks of melamine-fronted wall units. Made from stout planks or weathered old scaffolding planks that have been stripped and sanded, shelves can be used to store cookery books, attractive pieces of equipment and foodstuffs.

'Provide places for your things, so that you may know where to find them at any time, by day or by night,' Mother Ann Lee told the Shakers, who had storage down to a fine art. The built-in cupboards

in Shaker living quarters and workshops are the perfect illustration of their craft. These simple chests and cupboards had no extraneous detailing and were finely crafted in hardwoods with carefully graded proportions. Drawers, for instance, were often made smaller the higher up they were, so they were visually balanced as well as extremely practical, as heavier items could then be stored low down.

Freestanding cupboards were made on legs so that dust beneath could be swept away easily. Peg rails provided a place for hanging anything from chairs to brooms, mirrors, clocks and candle sconces. The Shakers would pack away many objects in lidded boxes. These beautiful and practical containers were crafted in a wide variety of shapes and sizes, so they were suited to almost any purpose. They would always be neatly stacked in order of size.

Small boxes in a variety of sizes were common in most country houses. They were used for the storage of all kinds of

household necessities – candles, food and spices, to name but a few. French country kitchens were furnished with ingenious storage receptacles, such as a *salière* (salt box) and a *panetière* (baguette box). In many households, handwoven baskets, crafted from reeds and rushes during the summer months, were used as storage receptacles for firewood and kindling.

Wall-mounted cupboards were also a common sight in rural dwellings. In the kitchen they were used to store food or cooking and eating utensils, while in the living room or parlour they housed important papers or perhaps the family bible. Those used to store foodstuffs can often be identified by their perforated or pierced fronts, which allowed fresh air to circulate while excluding insects and flies.

Nowadays, small wall-mounted cupboards made from odd bits of wood can be limed, painted or dressed with gingham to create a cheerful and useful addition to any room. Outmoded kitchen

equipment can be given a new lease of life. For example, pie safes and spit racks, dough boards, salt boxes and iron stands can all be transformed into items of storage, housing anything from books and magazines to toiletries and other bathroom paraphernalia.

Small cupboards and chests, brightly painted and displayed in appropriate places, are attractive pieces of folk art to be admired in their own right. But how much more satisfying it is to have something in your home that can actually be used rather than an object whose only function is decoration.

Easy country style does not mean cluttering up an interior with decorative bits and pieces, but it involves living with things that you love to have around you. Once it has been established exactly what is wanted and what can be thrown out, storage should no longer present a problem. Keep to a few fundamental rules: if you have items to display, display them well; otherwise, store them neatly in cupboards and firmly close the door.

When planning storage, leave room for expansion rather than building the storage around the possessions that you have now. Be generous with space and materials – thick, strong shelves are more satisfying to look at than thin, flimsy ones. Integrate your storage solutions into the overall style of the house. Even the most functional piece of furniture can be an attractive addition to a room.

textiles

Boldly patterned quilts, roughly woven checks, crisp starched cottons and fine embroidered linens – country textiles present a kaleidoscope of possibilities.

Handcrafted textiles, particularly quilts, are one of the principal ingredients of easy country style.

Since country-dwellers lacked the money and the opportunity to purchase rich patterned silks or heavy woven damasks, the majority spun their own textiles from natural materials – cotton, flax and wool. If fabrics were purchased, they were simple printed cottons and ginghams, used for dressmaking and home furnishings. Women were versed in the traditional skills of spinning, sewing, quilting and knitting, and often produced a family's clothes and linen single-handedly. Country living was a very frugal existence and fabric was always recycled and reused – worn sheets were given a new lease of life as snowy-white starched curtains, while old dresses, shirts and work overalls were cut up and put into the scrap box for patchwork quilts.

Quilts are the essence of American country style. Even the names of quilt designs are resonant of rural life: Rolling Rock, Honeycomb, Turkey Tracks, Bear's Paw, Flying Geese. Meanings varied from

Right An antique quilt is the starting point for a vibrant colour scheme.

Below A pile of woollen blankets makes a lively addition to a blue and white bedroom.

This page A group of blue and white American patchwork quilts illustrates the wide range of possible designs.

This page An antique red and white damask tablecloth bears a raised embroidery monogram. Ears of corn were a symbol of fertility, so this piece may have been part of a country girl's trousseau.

Above Drawn threadwork at the corners adds a touch of individuality to this linen panel. With its crochet-like finish at the top, it makes a lovely half-curtain that provides privacy without cutting out the light.

Above right Fine white handkerchief linen has been made up into a diaphanous Roman blind that allows diffused light to flood the room.

quilt to quilt, and a design would often reflect the stage in the quilter's life when it was made. Women collected scraps of fabric over many years, and each quilt would be a carefully constructed patchwork of memories, incorporating scraps from favourite dresses, children's clothes and curtains from the old home.

Life was hard for the pioneers, but quilting provided a creative outlet for many women, and the complexity and beauty of their quilts is amazing. It also provided a social focus – at a 'quilting bee' women would gather around a quilting frame with their neighbours and exchange news and gossip while they sewed. Antique country quilts are now

highly prized for their character and beauty and fetch large prices at auction, but the quilting tradition is a continuing one, with old patterns reworked and new ones still being invented, so cheaper modern quilts can also be found.

First and foremost, country fabrics are natural fabrics – cotton, linen and wool. Simple, boldly checked materials such as Shaker homespun, fresh cotton gingham and loosely woven Madras cotton are all redolent of comfortable, relaxed country style. Stripes have a similar appeal, while gauzy, translucent, light-filtering fabrics such as muslin, organza and cotton voile instantly evoke the artless and unadorned elegance of Swedish country style.

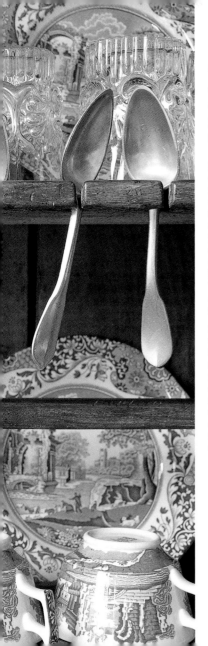

ceramics and tinware

The everyday tableware and kitchenware of the past has now become highly collectable. Functional design and unsophisticated finishes provide the key to Its current appeal.

Left Blue and white china grew popular in the 18th century, when quantities of it were imported from the Far East. Printed pastoral scenes such as these were fashionable in the 19th century. Their brightness and freshness suits country style.

Right American spatterware with its marble-effect glaze on tin was popular for everyday use in old country kitchens. Today these pieces are much sought after for their colour and decorative effect.

Ceramics and tinware have always been part of the country scene. Every country region had its own pottery vernacular – English earthenware and American redware are two examples; glazed with lead, they retained the colours of the earth. These types of pottery were fired at low temperatures and used for basic domestic items, but the fact that they are so rudimentary and close to the earth they came from makes them comforting objects to have around today.

Fired stoneware has its origins in the Rhine valley during the 15th century, when German potters discovered that

firing the local silaceous clay, or clay mixed with slate, at high temperatures created a dense ceramic material that was almost as hard as stone. When salt was added during the firing process, it formed a hard, long-lasting glaze. The technique for producing stoneware gradually filtered through Europe to England and from there to the New World. By the end of the 18th century, American stoneware had almost eclipsed earthenware in usage and popularity. In Britain, stoneware is most commonly associated with old-fashioned cider jars and hot-water bottles, while in the USA the production of stoneware is one of the country's most enduring traditions. Chunky utilitarian creamware, as it is known, remains a staple of diners and cafés all across the USA.

Enamelled tinware has similarly humble origins. In England, tin mugs were used as cheap drinking vessels by workers such as miners, while in France, red, blue and green glazed tinware is still on sale today in the form of cheap and cheerful pans, plates, mugs and coffee pots. Traditional American spatterware is a decorative form of tinware, often glazed with swirling marbled designs.

Whether they are new or old, part of a treasured collection or objects in daily use, tinware and ceramics have great decorative potential and careful thought should be given to their display. Old dressers are still the ideal backdrop for ceramics or china; the classic pairing of blue and white has a perennial appeal – and any collection of similar colours and designs will look good.

Top This chunky creamware jug epitomizes the pared-down look of modern country.

Above A shallow, wide pottery bowl such as this might have been used to pour milk into smaller bowls or cups.

Above left A hand-thrown kitchen bowl with a lovely creamy glaze on the inside demonstrates great integrity of style.

Opposite This rare collection of yellow-ware mixing bowls makes a dramatic impact in a simple kitchen cupboard.

rooms

Opposite This large country kitchen, painted cream and a calming blue-grey, is, in true country style, the heart of the home. To keep the room's sense of space and openness, there is a minimum of furniture, and what there is is on a large scale. Kitchen equipment, crockery and glass are stored away, leaving the work surfaces bare and uncluttered.

So far, this book has explored the various looks that make up easy country style, the traditional colours used in easy country homes, the different aspects of an easy country room – its floors, walls and furniture, its textiles and accessories. The next step is to combine all these elements so that every room in your home is a warm, welcoming and relaxing place to be. To do this, we must look to the past for inspiration, because it is the influence of the past that makes easy country style such a good antidote to today's stresses and strains. Our rural ancestors did not necessarily have easy lives, but they decorated their homes in a spirit of simplicity and resourcefulness which today manages to refresh the soul and uplift the spirit.

This page A kilim provides a brilliant splash of bold colour against the bleached wood, soft white walls and fabrics of this airy, uncluttered living room.

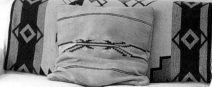

living rooms

To create an easy country living room, seek inspiration from the past and remember that colour, texture, warmth and a sense of peace are all essential elements of a welcoming living space.

Different rooms for different activities were rare in early country dwellings, and originally the living room was exactly what its name suggests – an area that was used for eating, sleeping and working in. It was not until the end of the 18th century that separate rooms were allocated for food preparation, eating and sleeping. Even then, many country dwellers continued to use the warm kitchen as the main living space and hub of the home.

Nowadays, many of us live in larger houses in busy urban areas and people commute to their places of work. We have more leisure time and our homes are primarily places for relaxation and rest. All these factors combine to make the modern living room a space that is devoted to comfort and companionship.

Light and space are the essential ingredients of an easy country living room. Put the emphasis on natural materials, comfort and order. Enhance natural light by using pale reflective colours. Choose low-contrast neutrals for a restful effect or bright naturals

Above Cottage windows and a low, beamed ceiling limit natural light in this living room. Pale walls and upholstery, sheer curtains and a well-placed mirror make the space seem larger and lighter.

that echo the world outside. Or team soft whites and creams with one bold shade to bring vitality to a simple space. If you are seeking to recreate a particular country style, the Colour and Surfaces section (pages 36–73) will help you to choose the right shades.

Using timber to cover a wall, in the form of panelling or tongue-and-groove cladding, creates a warm, natural effect.

Right The timber-plank walls of this 19th-century Texan farmhouse have been painted in the colours of the local landscape, making a wonderful backdrop for a collection of country antiques, which contribute to the room's simple, understated charm. There is no well-stuffed upholstered furniture to be seen, but the room seems warm and inviting.

This page The airy living room of a seaside home in Sweden proves the theory that less is more. The light wood panelling contributes to the room's nautical feel, while the curtainless windows give views of beautiful wooded countryside.

Left One-room living – the norm for country folk in the past – is reproduced in a barn conversion. Simple checked and floral fabrics reflect the country theme.

and choose simple checks and stripes in understated, elegant colours or finely woven linens and cottons.

The modern three-piece suite is not in tune with easy country style. Chairs and sofas need not match – simply dress them in loose covers in neutral shades, which can be removed for cleaning. Position seating to facilitate conversation and relaxation. If chairs are too far apart or ranged in a straight line, people will feel cut off. Coffee tables should not pose a barrier but be unobtrusive and functional. Two light, portable tray tables may be better than one heavy, low table.

Artificial light sources should be selected with comfort and ease in mind. A single overhead light source is not always the most flattering or practical solution, but if you feel it is necessary to retain an overhead light, the most appropriate fitting is a simply designed wrought-iron chandelier fitted with low-wattage bulbs.

To achieve an atmospheric, relaxing effect, choose uplighters or put lamps on side tables. Don't forget candles, the most authentic form of country lighting. They lend a sense of intimacy to any living room, and their dancing flames bring warmth and vitality.

If you are fortunate enough to have an open fireplace, a real log or coal fire is the ultimate in country hospitality, giving off a cosy glow and intermittent mesmeric blue flickers.

Alternatively, in a room that is being re-plastered, consider retaining the raw plaster as the wall finish – its faded tones have their own particular appeal.

In decorative terms, the floor provides the background for the rest of a room, so whatever flooring you prefer – stone, matting, wood or terracotta tiles – choose the best quality you can afford and look after it well, and you will be rewarded with a long-lasting floor that will develop a beautiful patina of age.

Even in a small room, a sense of spaciousness can be created by selecting furniture that harmonizes with the room's scale, installing built-in storage and dressing windows with blinds and simple curtains or slatted wooden shutters.

In dark interiors, you can enhance natural light with cleverly positioned mirrors – a mirror hung on a wall facing a small window will double the natural light in an interior. Avoid excessive use of pattern. Instead, imitate the Swedes

dining rooms

The days of formal dining with stiff-backed chairs, matching dinner sets and heavy, ornate silver cutlery are gone. The easy country dining room should be a comfortable, inviting space, home to an eclectic collection of rustic furniture.

Left Woodwork in Williamsburg blue makes a big impact when set against plain white walls in a pared-down rural dining room. The sturdy but sparse furnishings – rush-seated ladderback chairs and a gateleg oak table – suit the period and the style.

Below right Rough-hewn timber walls dominate the cosy dining room of a Kentucky log cabin. Along the wall stands an old food safe whose punched-tin door panels kept the flies away.

Country households rarely possessed a separate room for eating in. Meals were cooked and consumed in the kitchen, close to the warmth of the hearth. The concept of the dining room originated in Britain during the Georgian era, but only wealthy people with pretensions to fashion and style would have had such a room in their house. A dining room was something of a status symbol, enabling its owner to dine in splendour, while

being waited upon by a large retinue of servants. Meanwhile, country-dwellers continued to eat in the kitchen, as they had done for centuries.

Although the dining room may not be a particularly authentic country room, it is possible for modern dining areas to be decorated in an easy country style. A separate dining room is far from being considered a necessity these days. Many people eat their meals either in a large kitchen or at one end of an open-plan living room. Whatever form it takes, the dining area is all about setting the scene for conversation and companionship.

Dining rooms should be warm and inviting, but that doesn't necessarily

Above A wood pile and an informal bunch of flowers bring a country feel to this otherwise formal room.

Above left Painted American country furniture pieces stand out strongly in a plain room.

Left Floor-to-ceiling windows invite the outdoors into a dining space. Natural wood furniture and accessories reinforce the rural theme.

This page The Swedes have a knack of pairing elegance with rusticity to great effect. In this rural dining room, a rough fireplace contrasts with the crystal chandelier and plaster plaque.

Left Easy country interiors usually exclude clutter, but this kitchen/dining room in Provence manages to absorb it rather successfully. The predominance of white and cream unifies the busy mix of furniture and decorative objects.

Right A restored room in an old New England house has the warmth that only natural wood can provide. Pieces of furniture blend with the majestic fireplace and the wood panelling. The oil painting on the mantelpiece has been placed to one side to balance the small cupboard built into the wall and the asymmetrical fire surround.

dictate dark red or green walls, thick carpets and heavy brocade curtains. Simple wood panelling or cladding is especially welcome in an easy country-style dining room, but a coat of paint in a muted shade can also set a tranquil country mood. Choose soft whites or other pale hues in natural shades – moss or olive green, rosy terracotta, straw yellow, smoke blue.

Dining chairs need not match as long as they are all sturdy country shapes – for example, stalwart Windsor chairs will be at home alongside elegant rush-seated ladderbacks or a long trestle bench. A rustic farmhouse table looks good almost anywhere, and is practical and robust. If space is short, an old gateleg table with fold-up wings is ideal.

Once the practicalities have been catered for, concentrate on setting the scene. Create an intimate ambience with an informal chandelier over the table or dimmed electric lights supplemented with candles on the table.

Left and right An open-plan room in a Swedish waterside home has been designed to be as multi-functional as possible. The large central chimney houses an open fire with an antique fireback, as well as the cooking facilities – antique cast-iron doors have been added to modern appliances. The heat from the room warms a sleeping loft on the right-hand side, reached by a wooden ladder. Comfortable chairs provide a seating area, and another corner is lined with books and has a chair for quiet study or letter writing.

kitchens

Some country-style kitchens attract bric-a-brac and clutter, but easy country kitchens are characterized by simplicity, order and homeliness.

The country kitchen was always a busy, industrious place where women of different generations worked together to prepare and preserve food for the winter and feed the hungry farmer and labourers. It set the scene for many traditional country activities – washing, pickling, mending, weaving, preserving, butter- and cheese-making, baking.

On larger farms or in other country dwellings, different rooms were allocated for the purpose of different food-related tasks. For example, there might be a smokery, a dairy, a place to hang game, and, of course, a cool, dry pantry.

Natural, traditional materials are at the heart of the easy country kitchen. Flagstones, quarry tiles, granite or wooden floors feel solid underfoot and are easy to clean. A return to traditional carpentry techniques and woods has given us tables and chairs that are solid and substantial, work surfaces that you can really use without fear of damaging them, a roomy dresser that is worth the space it takes up rather than being a doll's house imitation of the real thing, and a butcher's block that you can chop on with gusto. In the same way, three or four sturdy, thick-bottomed pots and pans are worth more to the dedicated cook than a sparkling array of matching kitchenware that is scarcely used.

A worktop is another place where natural materials show their worth. Laminated plastic is not compatible with an easy country kitchen – instead, invest in tactile slate, polished marble, gleaming granite or warm, durable wood, all of which are hygienic, easy to clean, and will last a lifetime, their undeniable good looks only improving with age.

The archetypal country kitchen with its scrubbed table, open hearth and dresser conjures up an idyllic image of security and warmth. However, life in those kitchens was not always easy for our ancestors. Keeping them clean and warm was a daily struggle, and preparing

Top right The true craftsmanship of the Shakers is revealed in the detail.

Centre right Elegant reproduction Shaker chairs are well suited to easy country kitchens. Functional and lightweight yet solidly constructed, they will frequently survive many years of wear and tear.

Bottom right Roomy cupboards conceal prosaic bottles and tins, allowing work surfaces to be kept uncluttered.

Opposite A modern Shaker kitchen is true to one of the most important principles of Shaker design – that utility needs no ornament.

Opposite Hand-hewn, whitewashed wooden walls, painted furniture and traditional implements give character to an easy country kitchen. The barn-red paint used on the door, window frames and table, introduces splashes of colour. Homespun checked linen hangs at the window, while jugs and bowls are arranged on a set of freestanding shelves, rather than being dotted freely around the room.

Right This museum replica of an old American store has many elements of easy country style. The floor-to-ceiling drawers and shelves, with their display of sturdy kitchenware, are restrained and practical. Their blue-green colour is the perfect foil for the taupe earthenware. In the foreground, the simple wooden table, spread with a coarse cotton cloth, is laid with glass and cutlery from the museum's collection.

food without the benefit of modern labour-saving appliances – refrigerators, ovens, washing machines and dishwashers – was hard work indeed. Such appliances may not be picturesque, but they are still invaluable. In the easy country kitchen, they can be hidden behind wooden doors or stowed away in built-in cupboards. Alternatively, if you are lucky enough to have an old larder adjoining the kitchen, perhaps it could be converted into a utility room where these modern essentials can be concealed.

The easy country kitchen should be well equipped with a generous amount of storage and work space. Although fitted kitchens have fallen out of fashion in recent years, built-in cupboards remain the most space-effective answer to storage, especially in small kitchens, and they need not be ugly or expensive. They will neatly and economically make use of the entire wall space and can be custom-built around reclaimed elements such as an old sink, fireplace or kitchen range. Unpainted hardwood units are beautiful,

Above left and right and opposite Three different kitchens exemplify the pared-down country style. Ornate mouldings and door handles are replaced by unfussy panelled doors and utilitarian door furniture; walls are left plain; and accessories have an honest-to-goodness feel to them.

but MDF units painted with matt milk paint in authentic country colours such as rust, straw, buttermilk or green will also look the part. And, of course, one of the beauties of fitted cupboards and drawers is that they conceal all the tins, bottles and other paraphernalia that accumulate in every kitchen.

In a kitchen that is small and dark, try to avoid installing wall units, which can make the space feel even smaller and create a slightly claustrophobic effect. Instead, attach open shelves to the walls above the worktops to create a less 'fitted' and more informal effect. Use them to store items that are in frequent use, such as cookery books, mugs, sieves and pots and pans. Alternatively, kitchen utensils can be hung out of the way on a Shaker peg rail.

In many ways, an unfitted kitchen is more in keeping with the country style. Simple, freestanding cabinets, both old

and new, can be mixed and matched happily so an antique pine dresser will sit harmoniously alongside a gleaming, reconditioned 1950s Aga, an enormous Victorian butler's sink and a painted Hungarian armoire.

There are obvious advantages to an unfitted kitchen – not least the fact that the cabinets and cupboards can be taken with you when you move home. An unfitted kitchen is more versatile than a fitted one – furniture can be moved around as and when desired. An old wardrobe from the bedroom can be given a new lease of life as a cupboard for glassware and crockery. Or a large chest could be transferred from the kitchen to the bathroom and used to store towels and other household linens. Also, an unfitted kitchen will marry the old and the new to unusual effect. Your kitchen will be truly unique.

An easy country kitchen is a room to be lived in and enjoyed, a room that is redolent of warmth and relaxation, not a pristine, gleaming showroom. Not all kitchenware needs to be hidden away – a display of shining copper pots, country ceramics or baskets makes for a homely atmosphere. Old kitchen utensils such as copper jelly moulds and wooden spoons have a charm all of their own, but excessive amounts of kitchenware can be too much of a good thing – a few favourite pieces will have more impact than a jumble of items.

bedrooms

A bedroom should be a place of privacy and calm, somewhere to relax after a long, hectic day, so aim to create an atmosphere of simplicity and comfort that is conducive to rest and repose.

Sleeping arrangements in early country households were normally communal and extremely basic. A sleeping space might take the form of a straw-stuffed pallet thrown down at night in a shared living room, a narrow wooden bench, or the coffin-like box of a fold-out settle-bed. The first bedrooms consisted of beds built into the walls of cottages and screened with curtains or swinging doors. No doubt the occupants of these casement beds enjoyed their warmth and privacy, but today we might find them cramped and claustrophobic.

By the late 18th century, most country dwellings across Europe and America possessed a separate bedroom. People did not spend a great deal of time in their bedrooms – they were just for sleeping in – and as a result they were usually quite spartan, containing a bed, a washstand and a chest or chest of drawers for storing clothes and linen.

Windows were usually unscreened. Since country people rose and retired early, they had no need to block out the light. Creature comforts were few and far between – perhaps consisting of no more than a rag rug to protect the feet from cold floors and a warm, cosy quilt to keep out the winter chill.

Above Red and white toile de Jouy and floral fabrics give an understated feminine touch to an attic bedroom.

Above left Old wooden planking has been updated with an uneven blue stain that looks fresh and provides a perfect backdrop to a collection of blue and white fabrics.

Above all, an easy country bedroom should be conducive to relaxation and rest. For the walls, choose mild, calming hues that will create a soothing, tranquil atmosphere. Soft whites, delicate mint green, sunshine yellow or pale bird's-egg blue are all ideal choices. A bolder choice is wood panelling or cladding, which at once introduces a warm, reassuring and secure feel to any bedroom.

Floors should be kept uncluttered. In a room that has original floorboards hidden beneath carpet, tear up the carpet and sand, strip and wax or paint the boards to create a spacious and simple effect. If warmth and comfort is a priority, choose natural fibres such as jute or coir matting, with their characteristic uneven texture and warm hues. Cotton rugs are soft and warm beneath bare feet and come in muted colours.

Windows should be kept free from heavy lined and interlined curtains. Shutters will keep a room dark at night but allow light and air to flood in during the day. If you can tolerate a light room, choose thin, translucent roller blinds or blinds made from bamboo strips that can be raised and lowered with string. And, if you must have curtains, choose simple homespun or plain woven fabrics.

Artificial lighting in a bedroom should be soft, subdued and atmospheric. If you have not already done so, install a dimmer switch in your bedroom to make it possible to vary the level of lighting.

This picture
Antique twin beds
in a guest room are
high off the ground
to allow air to
circulate and to make
the floor easy to
clean. The quilts and
accessories are pure
American country,
while the kilim on
the floor pulls all the
colours together.

Left A pair of old quilts and a framed naive-style antique cot quilt define the colour scheme here. Everything else is simple: the unlined gingham curtains on tab headings, the striped sheets in a matching yellow and the rustic bedside table. The aqua-green walls sing with colour picked up from the quilts.

Right Ornately painted yellow beds make an unexpected but successful contrast with the utter simplicity of this bedroom. The plain ceiling rafters are painted white; the floor is made of white concrete with pebbles set into it; and the gingham bedspreads add a final down-to-earth touch to the room.

Gentle, glowing light that recalls the muted tones of candlelight and firelight is well suited to the easy country look.

Effective storage is very important if the aim is to create a simple, uncluttered easy country bedroom. Cupboards with adequate space for clothes and shoes enable you to shut the door on these things at night, and in the morning it is easy to find what you are looking for. Simple, well-crafted built-in cupboards make the most of the space available and, if they are painted the same shade as the walls, will contribute to a calming, clutter-free environment. Out-of-season clothes, clean and neatly folded, should be stored out of sight, while the things that are required every day should be kept within easy reach. Spare linen and towels should be tidily folded and stored away in a capacious armoire, old country chest or chest of drawers.

The easy country bedroom gives you an opportunity to indulge in textiles both old and new. Crisp, starched linen sheets, cool cotton pillow slips, warm blankets and cosy quilts all provide sensory delight and will transform a bedroom into a peaceful haven in which to awake refreshed every morning.

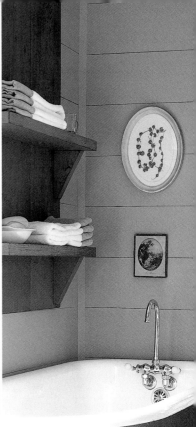

Above Wall planks of rough timber and irregular staining help to make this bathroom look rustic without sacrificing creature comforts.

Left A relaxed arrangement of accessories adorns an unusual stained-wood hanging shelf.

Right A freestanding roll-top bath with old chrome fittings takes centre stage in this bathroom, while small blue and white ceramic tiles give a gingham effect to the floor. The old stool, table and wide-panelled walls reinforce the easy country look.

bathrooms

Easy country bathrooms should be simple and functional, with a relaxed yet slightly utilitarian feel – but there is no need to sacrifice modern comforts.

Bathrooms are relatively recent additions to country houses. Before the arrival of mains water, country-dwellers made do with a pitcher of water, an outside toilet or earth closet, and a chamber pot, perhaps concealed in a cupboard.

The bathroom is one of the most functional rooms in the house, but it can also be a comfortable place to unwind. When you are planning a bathroom, the challenge is to strike a balance between modern practicality and a country style that is comfortable and relaxed.

The floor must be made of a material that will not be damaged by water. If you want the warmth of wood underfoot, the wood must be treated so that it will not warp and lift if water spills on it. Tiles are a practical choice – a chequerboard pattern, with its old-fashioned utilitarian air, is especially suitable, while terracotta tiles are evocative of Mediterranean warmth. However, in cooler northern climates, it may be desirable to provide something warm underfoot. Long cotton runners and traditional looped cotton bathmats all add comfort to hard floors and are simple to wash and dry.

This picture The ceiling of a small attic bathroom has been removed to expose the beams and the whole painted white to create a sense of space. The panelling extends above the bath to form a shelf.

Opposite A peg rail like this one, which holds a sponge bag and even a pair of bathroom cabinets, makes it easier to avoid clutter. Small wooden storage cabinets and chests are perfect for hiding medicines, cleaning fluids and plastic containers. The Shaker rocking chair with its woven seat and back and the cotton runner add comfort.

Absorbent finishes are effective in bathrooms since they make it possible for surfaces to breathe and do not encourage condensation. Plaster, either left unfinished or colour-washed in warm country colours, is ideal for country bathrooms. Tongue-and-groove provides a durable wall covering, especially when it is painted with microporous water-based paint especially formulated for bathrooms. Ceramic tiles are extremely water repellent, and you can indulge a love of colour with the jewel-like glazes of rustic tiles, especially those from Mexico and Spain.

The cast-iron roll-top bath is a fitting centrepiece for a country-style bathroom, setting the scene for a leisurely soak. Reconditioned roll-top baths can often be found in architectural salvage yards, which are also very good sources for traditional sinks and chunky old taps.

In a small bathroom, a roll-top bath may not be practical, but a simple white ceramic bath is also compatible with easy country style, especially if encased in tongue-and-groove or a panel cut from other natural materials – a slab of marble or slate, perhaps.

Country living suggests the luxury of taking a bath rather than a hasty shower in a cubicle, but you don't need to do without modern plumbing. Build an enclosed shower area around a drainage hole and tile it with vibrant ceramics – a solution that is both simple and practical.

porches

Originally, porches and verandas were intended to provide country-dwellers with protection against the elements, but they have developed into a space devoted to rest and relaxation.

Left On a hot Texan summer afternoon, what could be better than to relax on a shady porch beneath a cooling fan? The unusual collection of white-painted twig furniture with its soft cushions and fresh ticking covers offers a welcome respite from the heat of the sun, as do the crisp white walls and floor.

Right An unusual picket fence painted a buttery yellow to match the clapboard walls of the house gives this shady porch a private feel.

Country porches and verandas play a practical role, providing shade from the sun in hot countries and shelter from rain and snow in colder climates, but they also offer an opportunity for idyllic outdoor living, especially in warm summer months, when they function almost as an additional room.

In the USA, a wooden porch that runs the length of the house is a great institution. It serves as a place to read the morning newspaper, shell peas for lunch, or simply sit and watch the world go by, seated in a rocker by the screen door. The items found on a porch change with the changing seasons. In spring there

Far left A covered walkway between a house and a barn has been carefully laid with reclaimed cobblestones.

Left Bleached-out half-timbering looks stunning on the wall of a tall covered porch of an old French farmhouse.

Opposite An old weathered bench looks perfectly at home on the porch of a log cabin.

Below Porches on different sides of the house allow you to be in sun or shade, as you choose.

might be a few boxes of newly harvested vegetables; in summer a cluster of chairs will be grouped in the shade for after-lunch naps; in autumn it is adorned with pumpkins at Hallowe'en and bushels of dried corn at Thanksgiving; and in winter chopped wood sits in a neat pile, ready to be taken in for the fire.

In northern Europe, porches took the form of a covered shelter built around the front or back door of a house. They were primarily designed to offer some protection from the harsh elements, but they were also considered decorative additions to the façade of a house. Country-dwellers often whiled away

the hours on their porches in summer, and many porches had simple built-in benches at either side of the front door, rather like a church porch.

Porches and verandas can be painted in traditional country shades – barn red, soft green or ochre – or made more contemporary with daring bright colours. They also offer scope for imaginative outdoor furnishings, ranging from elegant wrought-iron garden furniture and wicker and rattan woven chairs to sturdy Adirondack chairs and tables, low benches and the ubiquitous rocking chair. Add a homely touch with plump, faded old cushions and covers.

resources

Where no address is given, call or visit the website for a store or stockist near you.

UK & USA

The Conran Shop
+ 44 (0)20 7589 7401
www.conran.com
+ 1 866 755 9079
www.conranusa.com
Modern furniture, fabrics, lighting and accessories.

Designers Guild
+ 44 (0)20 7351 5775
www.designersguild.com
+ 1 800 303 5413
www.designersguildus.com
Furniture, fabrics, wall coverings and accessories.

Farrow & Ball
www.farrow-ball.com
Historic paint colours and wallpapers.

Ikea
www.ikea.com
Scandinavian-style furniture and accessories at great prices.

Pierre Frey
www.pierrefrey.com
French weaves, cottons, linens and prints.

Ralph Lauren Home
www.ralphlaurenhome.com
Homewares that combine rusticity and elegance.

MAINLY UK

Cath Kidston
+ 44 (0)20 7221 4000
www.cathkidston.co.uk
Vintage fabrics and furniture.

Colefax & Fowler
+ 44 (0)20 7493 2231
www.colefax.com
Traditional English country house prints, weaves, plains and wallpapers.

The Dining Room Shop
64 White Hart Lane, Barnes
London SW13 OPZ
+ 44 (0)20 8878 1020
www.thediningroom
shop.co.uk
Antique and reproduction dining tables, chairs, china and accessories.

Habitat
+ 44 (0)8444 99111
www.habitat.net
Modern furniture, fabrics and accessories.

Ian Mankin
109 Regents Park Road
London NW1 8UR
+ 44 (0)20 7722 0997
www.ianmankin.com
Stripes and checks in cotton and linen.

Lacquer Chest
75 Kensington Church Street
London W8 4BG
+ 44 (0)20 7937 1306
www.lacquerchest.com
Antique country furniture and accessories.

Plain English Design
Stowupland Hall
Stowupland
Stowmarket
Suffolk IP14 4BE
+ 44 (0)1449 774028
www.plainenglishdesign.co.uk
Simple bespoke country kitchens and furniture.

The Stencil Library
Stocksfield Hall
Stocksfield
Northumberland NE43 7TN
+ 44 (0)1661 844844
www.stencil-library.com
Comprehensive stencils.

Tobias & the Angel
68 White Hart Lane
Barnes
London SW13 OPZ
+ 44 (0)20 8878 8902
www.tobiasandtheangel.com
Antique and reproduction country furniture and fabrics.

MAINLY USA

Aged Woods, Inc.
2331 East Market Street
York, PA 17402
+ 1 800 233 9307
www.agedwoods.com
Antique heart pine, ash, hickory and other unusual domestic flooring.

Benjamin Moore Paints
www.benjaminmoore.com
A selection of period-style colours in muted shades.

Calico Corners
+ 1 800 213 6366
www.calicocorners.com
Over 100 retail outlets that discount top-quality fabrics.

Country Curtains
+ 1 413 298 5565
www.countrycurtains.com
A wide selection of curtains, sheers and door panels.

Cowtan & Tout
www.cowtan.com
Furnishing textiles by Colefax & Fowler, Cowtan & Tout, Larsen, Jane Churchill, Manuel Canovas.

Crate and Barrel
+ 1 800 967 6696
www.crateandbarrel.com
Good-value furniture and accessories.

The Demolition Depot & Irreplaceable Artifacts
216 East 125th Street
New York, NY 10035
+ 1 212 860 1138
www.demolitiondepot.com
Period doors, shutters, mantels, stone and terracotta pieces, and other architectural salvage.

Keepsake Quilting
PO Box 1618
Center Harbor, NH 03226
+ 1 800 525 8086
www.keepsakequilting.com
A good selection of lightweight cottons.

MAINLY USA

Aged Woods, Inc.
(see above)

The Old Fashioned Milk Paint Company
436 Main Street
Groton, MA 01450
+ 1 978 448 6336
www.milkpaint.com
Paints made from natural pigments that replicate the colour and finish of Colonial and Shaker antiques.

Old Village Paints
+ 1 800 498 7687
www.old-village.com
Authentic colour reproductions from the Colonial, Federal and Victorian periods.

Palacek
+ 1 800 274 7730
www.palacek.com
Manufacturers of fine wicker, rattan and wood furniture.

Paris Ceramics
+ 1 212 644 2782
www.parisceramics.com
Limestone, terracotta, stone, and hand-painted tiles.

Pottery Barn
+ 1 212 219 2420
www.potterybarn.com
Contemporary furniture and accessories for the home.

Restoration Hardware
www.restoration
hardware.com
Fine hardware, furniture, and home accessories.

Ruby Beets Old & New
25 Washington Street
Sag Habor, NY 11963
+ 1 631 899 3275
www.rubybeets.com
Vintage and contemporary furniture and accessories.

West Elm
+ 1 888 922 4119
www.westelm.com
New retail chain offering contemporary furniture and a wide range of homewares.

index

*Figures in italics refer
to captions.*

publisher's acknowledgments

Ryland Peters & Small would like to thank all the people who kindly allowed us to photograph their homes for this book, including JoAnn Barwick and Fred Berger; Bill Blass; Zara Colchester; Chris and Julia Cowper; Mr and Mrs Robin Elverson; Katie Fontana and Tony Niblock; Wendy Harrop; Vera and Manrico Iachia; Beverly Jacomini; Bruno and Hélène Lafforgue; Susan and Jerry Lauren; Lena Proudlock; Mr and Mrs Derald Ruttenberg; and Liz Shirley.

author's acknowledgments

Making the original edition of this book, first published in 1998, was a total pleasure, not only on account of the team who were involved, but also because the subject is where my heart lies.

Many thanks to Simon Upton for his strong and honest photographs; to Jacqui Small for her abundant wisdom; to Anne Ryland and David Peters for their continued support; to Larraine Shamwana and Maggie Town for their design expertise; to Annabel Morgan for her calm and efficient editing; to Alison Culliford for pulling the text together with speed and elegant accuracy; and to all at Ryland Peters & Small who are involved in the complicated business of making books.

Many thanks also to all those people who let us photograph their homes, and to the architects and designers who helped to make those homes so special. We were well looked after everwhere, but special thanks go to Beverly Jacomini, whose infectious spirit and style accompanied us in Texas and Kentucky, where her design work perfectly exemplifies Easy Country; also to Delores Gummelt, whose humour saw us through the Texas summer heat; to Al McGloin at Bill Blass's house for kind hospitality and the best hamburgers on earth; to Anna Liisa Russell in Pennsylvania for her kindness and enthusiasm; to Delena Crawford for her homemade cookies; to Julie Saetre at the Conner Prairie Museum for all her help.

As always, a big thank you to David, my husband, and our son, Harry, for putting up with all the absences.

business credits

key: a=above, b=below, r=right, l=left, c=centre.

Bruno & Hélène Lafforgue
Mas de l'Ange
Maison d'Hôte
Petite route de St Remy-de-Provence
13946 Mollégès, France
Pages 54–55, 57bl, 60, 61 both, 69, 81ar, 92, 93ar, 94ar, 104ar, 118, 133.

Conner Prairie
open-air living-history museum
13400 Allisonville Road
Fishers, Indiana 46038
USA
+ 1 800 966 1836
www.connerprairie.org
Pages 38–39, 58al, 66, 71bl, 74, 77, 79a, 86b, 93al, 93br, 94b, 95 both, 102–103, 124, 125, 140bl.

Chris Cowper
Cowper Griffith Associates
chartered architects
15 High Street
Whittlesford
Cambridge CB2 4LT
+ 44 (0)1223 835998
www.cowpergriffith.co.uk
Pages 32–35, 47, 50, 51r, 140al.

Ecomusée de la Grande Lande
Marquèze
40630 Sabres, Bordeaux
France
www.parc-landes-de-gascogne.fr
Pages 2, 4–5, 62ar, 76al, 76br, 80 inset, 140ar.

Jacomini Interior Design
1701 Brun Street, Suite 101
Houston, Texas 77019
USA
tel + 1 713 524 8224
fax +1 713 524 0951
www.jacominidesign.com
Pages 3, 10, 40l, 43, 52–53a, 53r, 56, 57r, 58bl, 67, 68l, 71al, 76bl, 81bl, 87 main, 89, 98a, 103r, 115, 128, 129l, 132–33, 138–39.

JoAnn Barwick Interiors
P.O. Box 982
Boca Grande, Florida 33921
USA
Pages 40–41, 42, 68c, 88bl, 91al, 105, 113 inset.

Lena Proudlock
www.lenaproudlock.com
Pages 24–27, 45 both, 46bl, 64–65, 82l, 84–85, 90a, 106, 116ar, 117.

Maximilian Lyons
Lyons+Sleeman+Hoare
Nero Brewery
Cricket Green
Hartley Wintney, Hook
Hampshire RG27 8QA
+ 44 (0)1252 844144
www.lsharch.co.uk
Pages 62bl, 126r.

Nancy Braithwaite Interiors
2300 Peachtree Road, Suite C101
Atlanta, Georgia 30309
USA
tel + 1 404 355 1740
fax + 1 404 355 8693
Pages 51l both, 68r, 79br, 80 main, 82r, 91br, 101r, 116al, 134 both, 134–135.

Ocke Mannerfelt design
Hamnvägen 8
183 51 Täby
Sweden
+ 46 8 756 03 60
www.ocke.se
Pages 36, 39r, 72al, 78 both, 79bl, 112–13, 120–21, 121.

Plain English cupboardmakers
Stowupland Hall
Stowupland
Stowmarket
Suffolk IP14 4BE
+ 44 (0)1449 774028
www.plainenglishdesign.com
Pages 7, 48l both, 62br, 91ar, 104br, 122, 123, 126l, 127.

Vera Iachia interior design
Rua das Flores, n°105–2'Esq
1200–194 Lisboa
Portugal
+ 351 21 387 33 71
www.veraiachia.com
Pages 20–23, 46a, 46br, 72br, 88a.

Winedale Historical Center
P.O. Box 11, Round Top, Texas 78954
USA
Page 73.